GRAPHIC CONNECTIONS IN ARCHITECTURE

rsmdesign

VISUAL PROFILE BOOKS, NEW YORK

Published by:
Visual Profile Books, Inc.
389 Fifth Avenue, New York, NY 10016
Phone: 212.279.7000
www.visualprofilebooks.com

Distributed by:
National Book Networks, Inc.
15200 NBN Way, Blue Ridge Summit, PA 17214
Toll Free (U.S.): 800.462.6420
Toll Free Fax (U.S.): 800.338.4550
Email orders or Inquiries: customercare@nbnbooks.com

ISBN 13: 978-1-7330648-7-3

Library of Congress Cataloging in Publication Data:
RSM Design
www.rsmdesign.com

Printed and bound in China

TABLE OF CONTENTS

GRAPHIC CONNECTIONS
LEGACY MEMORIES

BY RONALD ALTOON, FAIA

CREATING A FRAMEWORK

As an architect and designer, I am a contextualist not only by formal education, but also by natural instinct, inclination, and consequence. It seems to be the only ecologically responsible ethic to espouse. Accordingly, I define context in the most holistic terms as it manifests different influences in every location, for every people, at every moment in time.

Contextual forces inform design choices ranging from overarching concepts to minute details. They set the framework for what ultimately defines us as who we are. Response to these forces affix a design into its setting either effectively or awkwardly. They are perhaps subconsciously, but certainly and inescapably detected by those who will form an affinity with or an irritation from what engages them in the most intimate and personal ways. It is these very forces which imbue memory.

- Natural Forces of sun, wind, precipitation, and humidity affect human comfort.

- Geographic Forces of geology, topography, landscape, and water influence integration with nature.

- Historic Forces of natural resources, tectonics, vernacular architecture, and craft define legacy of place.

- Urban Forces of planning and zoning criteria, building codes, utility infrastructure, roadway network, transportation systems, and sustainability mandates define constraints and opportunities.

- Physical Forces of site configuration, access/egress, building massing, and adjacencies influence disposition of a program on a specific site.

- Human Forces of politics, economics, religion, social structure, and culture define community.

- Market Forces of competition, demographics, psychographics, and catchment area create opportunity and possibility.

- Digital Forces of omni-channel access redefine engagement between the retailer/hotelier/restauranteur/entertainer and the customer.

THINKING CONTEXTUALLY

How, then, does one effectively respond to these forces? A contextually influenced architect seeks to hear direct voices from the past and present to determine if precedent should inform or even drive the conception of appropriate design responses. Engineers justify their creations as they are brought into physical reality, generally in the most efficient manner. They are very good at that.

Taken together, this creates the physical equivalent of prose in literature. All the objective elements are there—nouns, adjectives, verbs, adverbs, and prepositional phrases, necessary to construct a cogent text. But what instills the heartbeat? And, what gets it ticking? In literary terms, where are the poetics sourced?

One might make the case that the architect's vision is enhanced measurably by the complimentary skills of additional design (rather than engineering) professionals who complete the chorus of voices necessary to create both harmony and dissonance and, in particular, to imbue memory. The urban designer's hardscape elements and furnishings, the landscape architect's site-specific water features and plant selections, the art consultant's curating of artists and media, the architectural lighting designer's enhancement effects, and the environmental graphic designer's keen eye for the obvious, obscure, and ingenious enrich the mix and create engagement with people in ways that touch their hearts and build community.

The most visible of these expressions is seen in the fingerprints of the environmental graphic design firm. They most clearly take their cues from the natural environment, historic precedent, physical setting, and social and cultural forces. They, more than any, understand the imprint of not only the demographic profile within a particular trade area, but also the psychographic presence which separates desire from need, enjoyment from errands, self-esteem from simply being. They bring transcendence. That is their stock in trade.

PERSONAL

I was first introduced to the partners of Redmond Schwartz Mark Design not long after they were established in 1997. Martin Schwartz and Harry Mark were classmates in the School of Architecture at the University of Texas in Austin and brought an understanding of both the architects thought process and design values. Suzanne, Martin, and Harry had all worked together at RTKL in Dallas, and upon forming RSM Design were introduced to my firm, Altoon Partners (formerly Altoon + Porter Architects), by a former graphic design associate of ours who had migrated to Disney Imagineering where she interacted favorably with them.

Over the years we have collaborated with RSM Design on over 40 projects, both international and domestic. With sites throughout the United States, in Eastern Europe and Asia, their acute sensitivities to the forces of context to inform their thinking seemed most simpatico with our own. It was a harmonious fit. Every time they brought joy to their work, their relationships, and the communities benefitted from their senses.

Educated as architects, Martin and Harry understood architects and their inclinations. But they were uncommonly able to isolate their architectural instincts effectively so as to pose really insightful questions without appearing to intrude into the architect's design psyche. Architects, genetically over-protective of their intellectual territory, are easily threatened, and mostly intolerant of intrusions into their inner sanctum of ideas. Harry and Martin skillfully navigated these treacherous seas, while Suzanne deftly introduced complimentary ideas into the mix generally not considered by architects as possibilities. Their unique alchemy of curiosity, creativity, and collaboration effected the perfect prescription for every situation.

RSM DESIGN

Over five decades of practice, I've engaged and worked collaboratively with a host of highly skilled two-dimensional (paper) graphic designers and three-dimensional environmental graphic design firms. Among them were Saul Bass, Deborah Sussman of Sussman Prejza & Associates, and Henry Beer of Communication Arts. All were gifted, talented, energetic and skilled designers. Without a doubt, the most natural fit for the work of Altoon Partners, the firm which stood apart as possessing the most alluring elixir of creative and professional engagement, was RSM Design.

A highly engaging firm, collegial, impossible to rattle with severe criticism, they always came to the challenge with optimism and interest. And, they listened well. All designers are blessed with large egos. Those at RSM Design channel theirs to achieve the client's vision, contributing their part to achieve the desired outcome. This is, for certain, a value-added proposition.

Having worked directly with the San Clemente, Dallas, and Los Angeles offices, I find it remarkable that their company culture transcends geography, and translates into the hearts of every individual, on every project, and for every place. To a person they bring a level of energy, excitement, curiosity, and creativity rarely exhibited by environmental graphic design professionals. Their passion is infectious, obvious from the outcome. They are consummate professionals and wonderful friends.

RONALD ALTOON, FAIA

Throughout a nearly 50-year professional career, working in several distinguished architectural practices and leading his own firm for 30 years, Ronald Altoon, FAIA has led the design efforts on a myriad of project types, achieving award-winning design recognition. He continues to guide the architectural profession while serving on a number of influential boards and foundations, and was the National President of The American Institute of Architects in 1997. Ronald has lectured at over 25 university schools of architecture, art history, business, real estate development, law, and liberal arts.

RSM Design has been fortunate to collaborate with Ronald Altoon on over 40 projects around the world. A few projects of note include: Victoria Gardens, Rancho Cucamonga, CA; LAX Gateway, Los Angeles, CA; The Paseo, Pasadena, CA; Waikiki Beach Walk, Honolulu, HI; Downtown Summerlin, Las Vegas, NV; Moskva Collection, Moscow, Russia; Metallist City Centre, Kharkiv, Ukraine; Central World, Bangkok, Thailand; Marina City, Qingdao, China.

FINDING PLACE
THE PRACTICE OF RSM DESIGN

_____

BY JAMES BURNETT, FASLA

How we navigate through space is an eternal challenge for designers—from the city-making plans of the ancient Romans where the public functions were demarcated and celebrated—to our modern cities where the cacophony of buildings, landscape and networked systems of place work together in noisy symphonies. In the last quarter century, we have become more attuned to the idea of placemaking as a form of design language, but this often presupposes that there was no place signifier at the start.

RSM Design, in a body of richly conceived and executed projects across the globe, is a rare collective of designers who look deeply at place, not as a tabula rasa, but as a palimpsest for the cues to connect people to place and to connect people to each other. So, while placemaking helps them to amplify the culture, site and people, they also embrace their role as placekeepers, a team that listens keenly and through many different lenses, to build places where memory and community are the threads that ground us. More completely and more accurately, however, RSM Design is interested in place-finding—the true and authentic experience found in layers of history, experience, people and time.

OJB Landscape Architecture has had the good fortune to be collaborators with RSM Design on a wide variety of projects and in settings ranging from large urban parks and children's

playgrounds to innovative mixed-use districts. Many collaborations later, the common thread is RSM Design's ability to unearth the story of the site, the community and the purpose in every undertaking. Our long history together can be understood, in no small measure, by the way RSM Design is committed to blurring the boundaries between disciplines to help inform a better understanding of our built (and unbuilt) environment.

At LeBauer Park in Greensboro, North Carolina, for instance, RSM Design used environmental graphic design to help create a public park designed as a diverse series of garden and plaza spaces. With signage that announced the playful identity of the park, the immediate message was one of celebration and discovery and became a regional icon. Color is also used as a welcoming device, helping to create movement through the dynamic new park. That park is much better because of RSM's design that set the tone and feeling for those spaces.

Embracing this dialogue can be traced to the founding principals of the firm: Suzanne Redmond Schwartz, Martin Schwartz and Harry Mark, each with diverse and complementary backgrounds in architecture, site design, graphics, color, business and branding. The intersection between architecture, landscape and environment informs every project, and is truly part of their DNA.

RSM Design also understands materiality, and how the transition from one space to another is informed by the alchemy of stone, water, earth, light, wind, plants, and trees as people move through them. Navigating through these visual cues can help tell the story of the site. Day and night, season to season, these markers change and transform. In many of their projects, high tech is married with high touch. At its heart, this philosophy puts people first. RSM Design creates spaces that are finely tuned and are well crafted, and they make a statement with their designs; one that captures the spirit of place, is a wow experience and most importantly has a feeling of optimism.

JAMES BURNETT, FASLA

Founding The Office of James Burnett (OJB) in 1989, James has dedicated his career to creating meaningful spaces that challenge the conventional boundaries of landscape architecture. OJB has garnered over eighty state and national design awards. Throughout his work, there has been a particularly strong focus on designing landscapes that promote healthy living, focusing on the transformation of American cities through the creation of active public spaces. In 2004 Jim was made a Fellow by the American Society of Landscape Architects, the highest form of honorary recognition that the professional association can bestow upon one of its members, and in 2016 was awarded the ASLA Design Medal. In 2020 OJB was awarded the National Design Award for Landscape Architecture by the Cooper Hewitt, Smithsonian Design Museum.

RSM Design has been fortunate to collaborate with James Burnett on over 16 projects around the United States. A few projects of note include: Missouri Riverfront Revitalization, Omaha, NE; Hollywood & Highland, Los Angeles, CA; LeBauer Park, Greensboro, NC; CityLine, Richardson, TX; The Drew, Las Vegas, NV; Hughes Landing, The Woodlands, TX; Playa Vista, Los Angeles, CA.

THE NEIGHBORHOOD.
THE TOWN CENTER.
THE PARK.
THE SCHOOL.
THE MUSEUM.

These are destinations that hold a special place in our hearts. They are the places that people return to again and again. They are the soul of the community, the anchors for memories and the spaces for inspiration or learning. Creating that kind of special place requires a vision which combines an appreciation of the human experience and a clear understanding of the built environment.

There are no templates in creating places that people truly love; every place and project is unique. Each place offers insights into different cultures, uses or perspectives that require their own original recipe for design. It is essential for architectural graphic designers to translate the unique character and qualities of a place with relevance, resonance and inspiration.

DESIGN AS A BRIDGE

THE PSYCHOLOGY OF UNCONSCIOUS CONNECTIONS

The psychology of design is an essential ingredient in connecting people to place. More than simply decorating the side of a building, architectural graphic design is critical to establishing the purpose of a space, the visitor's place within it, and helping to shape the overall experience. While one may never recognize that design is at play, the work architectural graphic designers do, when done well, is essential to establishing that unconscious connection.

Architectural graphic design is about creating a vocabulary of design elements that reinforces the architecture and helps define the context for a place that people will connect with. Subtleties in design can have a huge impact. A different typeface can completely change the vibe of a place. A well-placed bench can bring moments of comfort. A unique graphic can inspire selfies in the parking lot. These are the emotional connections that drive people, the unconscious aspects that create resonance and transform a visit into an experience. This is the art of architectural graphic design at its most powerful.

The creative work of the design team is the transformative process that turns bricks, glass, steel, and concrete into a place with soul and style. It's mission is to create places for people to linger, guide them to new destinations, and facilitate shared experiences. Design is greater than an aesthetic overlay. It goes beyond making a space look good to expressing the essence of a place and profoundly connecting it to the people that will inhabit and visit the place.

Designers have a broad palette to work with—identity, typography, symbols, materials, colors, signage, wayfinding, public art—all the tools needed to root the environment in it's place and make it meaningful to each person whom experiences it. The goal is to forge a subconscious connection by building an immersive experience that resonates more deeply than words.

The purpose behind architectural graphic design is at the intersection of the grandeur of architecture and the beauty of the human spirit. And it's this unique blend that poses the best challenges and inspires thoughtful and creative design solutions.

DESIGN TRANSFORMS BRICKS, GLASS AND CONCRETE INTO A PLACE WITH SOUL AND STYLE

WE CANNOT
CONTROL
THE WIND
But
WE CAN
ADJUST
THE SAILS

Shops

Shops

Front

NEWPORT BEACH, CA EST. 1942

LIDO MARINA

VILLAGE

ENGAGING THE PHYSICAL SPACE

THE PHYSICAL SPACE AND THOSE WHO EXPERIENCE IT

In the simplest terms, architectural graphic design is about marrying the elements of architecture to the needs of the people that will experience it. Every connection to a built environment starts with the physical space and the context.

The disciplines of architecture and graphic design live harmoniously and symbiotically together. This relationship has been around for centuries as an important component of the project narrative. Whether through hieroglyphics, classical inscriptions, façade stenciling, strong building identities, the two disciplines work together to create a cohesive narrative of the building and the way the visitor interacts with it. This marriage is not limited to buildings alone, but also manifests itself in civic spaces and urban places where signage, wayfinding, and art combine to create richness, character, functionality, and engagement.

Architecture speaks of space, form, place, and function while architectural graphic design communicates a building's function, purpose, message, and narrative. Effective and appropriate architectural graphic designs support the statement made by a building and strengthen its presence. The graphics layered into the environment are derived from the architectural context, spatial context, cultural context, and historical context to which they relate. They are not independent nor superficial. The design elements provide meaning, form, function, and purpose, along with the architecture. Whether these architectural graphic designs are woven into the building or space through identity signage, wayfinding signage, specialty features, or graphic embellishments, there is an open dialogue that mutually benefits one another.

Architectural graphic design creates a strong sense of place, fulfills human needs, helps users find their way, and communicates a building's narrative, fostering a strong connection between the person and place. The relationship of architecture and graphic design is a symbiotic alliance that orients, informs, and delights.

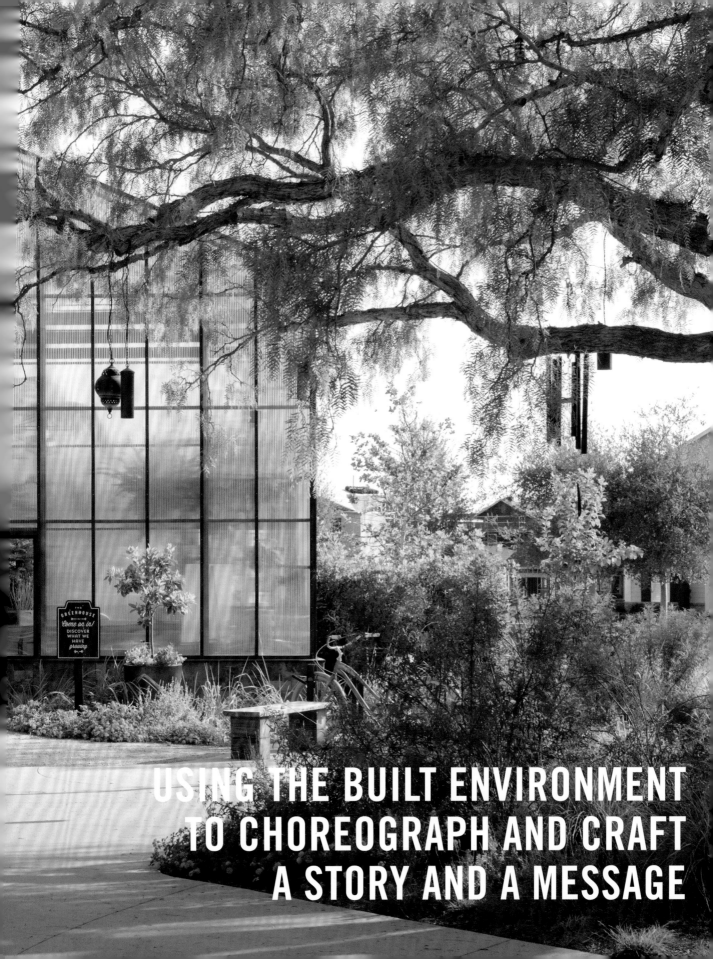

USING THE BUILT ENVIRONMENT
TO CHOREOGRAPH AND CRAFT
A STORY AND A MESSAGE

IT'S ALWAYS ABOUT PEOPLE

A PRINCIPLE-CENTERED DESIGN APPROACH

The primary guiding principle of successful environmental graphic design is that people are at the center of everything. Whether thinking of people in terms of individuals, groups, or communities, they are inherently at the center of the designer's work. The intention behind any project is to get people to feel good, to give them a sense of meaning in place, and to help them identify within an environment so they can build that lasting connection.

When visitors look at a place, drive up or walk through it, the work of architectural graphic designers is what helps make it recognizable, and more importantly resonant. People should feel good about putting their energy into this place, to being a part of it.

The idea is that people should feel empowered by the spaces they occupy. So, how does the designer invigorate the environment to make it more engaging and create the kinds of connections that surpass the physical?

By placing people at the center of the design process. Everything revolves around understanding the core needs, values, and objectives of the people that will occupy the space. It is all about their motivations and desires. Brands, wayfinding, signage, and artful moments engage the psychology, spark memories, tap emotions. It has become apparent over the years that subtleties in design, a different typeface, color choices, the placement of a piece of art can totally transform the experience.

Places have the power to become a part of a person's identity; particularly when they when they stand for something meaningful. Making that connection requires a deeper level of sensitivity and understanding. A colorful sign will not do it. To be effective, the work has to engage at every human level—the body, the mind, the heart, and the spirit.

PRINCIPLE-CENTERED DESIGN

The work is guided by a principle-centered approach that
is committed to engaging people into the design process
and ultimately, to the environments that are created.

PEOPLE

Integrate a people first approach
through empathetic understanding,
engagement and alignment to
co-create insightful design solutions

① ③ ②

DESIGN

Create unique design
solutions that connect
people to the built
environment through
meaningful experiences

PROCESS

Utilize an inside-out
holistic approach that
follows a disciplined
methodology to generate
innovative results

STIN LEGACY

TO BE TRULY EFFECTIVE
THE DESIGNS HAVE TO ENGAGE AT
EVERY HUMAN LEVEL—THE BODY,
THE MIND, THE HEART AND THE SPIRIT

MAKING HOLISTIC CONNECTIONS

THE MOTIVATIONS OF THE WHOLE PERSON

As architectural graphic designers, every new project is rich with opportunities to help connect people to places. Not only is the designer mindful of the multiple intelligences that motivate people wherever they may venture, but the Design Leadership Process is governed by principles that truly put people at the center of every design decision.

By tapping into each of the intelligences below, designers aim to create places and experiences that are mindful of the whole person. Creating a holistic connection of people to place is the ultimate goal by utilizing a process that follows these same four motivations.

IQ

MENTAL INTELLIGENCE
Creating environments that encourage people to think and mentally engage with a place. Information plaques and signage as well as historical markers help facilitate mental engagement.

VISION
Knowing what the right things to do are before doing them right.

SQ

SPIRITUAL INTELLIGENCE
Connection to ideas bigger than one's self and the ability to think creatively beyond what is seen and experienced on a daily basis. The desire to seek purpose and meaning, and to have accountability in what we design.

CONSCIENCE
Crafting solutions based on principles & values.

PQ

PHYSICAL INTELLIGENCE
Creating places that encourage connection with the environment through physical engagement. Wayfinding signage helps people navigate and engage in their environments and encourages physical mobility.

DISCIPLINE
The end pre-exists in the means... the process will determine the product.

EQ

EMOTIONAL INTELLIGENCE
Creating environments that invite communication and social interaction with others. Placemaking elements and specialty graphics enrich the environment and encourage emotional connections.

PASSION
Creating places people love.

MOTIVATIONS OF THE WHOLE PERSON

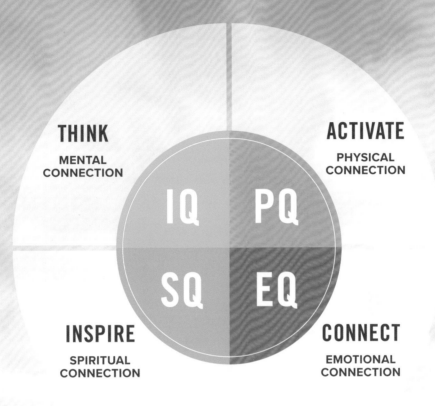

THINK
MENTAL CONNECTION

ACTIVATE
PHYSICAL CONNECTION

IQ PQ

SQ EQ

INSPIRE
SPIRITUAL CONNECTION

CONNECT
EMOTIONAL CONNECTION

THE PRINCIPLES OF CERTAINTY, VARIETY AND DELIGHT CONNECT PEOPLE TO PLACE THROUGH A LAYERED EXPERIENCE

CREATING A MEANINGFUL LAYERED EXPERIENCE

CERTAINTY

Creating a sense of comfort, security and familiarity

BRAND / LOGO
MONUMENTATION / IDENTITY
WAYFINDING / DIRECTIONAL SIGNS

VARIETY

Creating a reason to discover and explore

PLACEMAKING
DISTRICTING / TENANT SIGNAGE
PROGRAMMING / EVENTS

DELIGHT

Creating places of surprise and enjoyment

ART PROGRAMS / MURALS
SPECIALTY GRAPHICS
EDUCATION PROGRAMS

A MEANINGFUL LAYERED EXPERIENCE

CERTAINTY, VARIETY, DELIGHT

Abraham Maslow is best known for his 1943 paper, "A Theory of Human Motivation," where he establishes and outlines the five basic human needs. At the bottom of the famous pyramid are the physiological needs, the most basic necessities for human life—food, water, air, shelter, and clothing, to name a few. This is followed by the need for safety, then the need for love and belonging, then esteem (self-respect and feeling respected by others), and at the very top of the hierarchy is the need for self-actualization.

It is important to take all of these human needs into consideration when designing, because they are fundamental principles that connect people to places they will feel comfortable and fulfilled, and ultimately want to spend time in again and again. When viewed alongside the design process, Maslow's Hierarchy of Needs fits seamlessly into the design of a place. It is called "Certainty, Variety, Delight," and is concentrated on these three elements to simplify and focus the design intent for every project to create a rich, layered experience rooted in human needs.

Nobody likes feeling lost or not knowing what to do in unfamiliar situations. **Certainty** taps into this idea, that when you are going to a new place, you should be provided ample direction to be confident in your ability to navigate the space. This is the foundation of the pyramid: providing people with the right information, at the right time.

The paradox at the core of this need for certainty is that too much comfort and too much security can create a sense of predictability and boredom. People stop engaging with their surroundings and instead move blindly through the space between their destinations.

Variety provides that little change of pace—enough difference to keep you in the moment and create an awareness of the details of their surroundings. It breaks the rhythm of a place and allows for moments of exploration, curiosity, and learning.

Creating moments of **delight** is one of the most challenging aspects of the design process. To truly be delightful, the moment can not feel forced or contrived; it must occur naturally and organically, and above all, it must make people happy. These are the moments that show the true personality, culture, and history of a project, and the moments that turn into memories.

CONNECT

CONNECTING PEOPLE TO PLACE THROUGH STORYTELLING, CULTURAL CONTEXT & HERITAGE

Storytelling is a universal way to connect people to place, building bridges that tie people together to the places where they gather. Stories set the stage to foster community and commonality when these narratives are woven throughout a project, connecting people to place. Emotional connections can be built through big impactful moments as well as through small thoughtful details.

Connecting people to place can have a rich emotional component as people call a place their own, consider places as an extension of their identity and strongly connect with the history of a place. The work of the designer enhances connections by utilizing branding and placemaking components as opportunities to enrich the overall experience amd build emotional and social ties with an environment.

CASE STUDY

MIAMI DESIGN DISTRICT

MIAMI, FLORIDA

TRANSFORMING AN UNDERUTILIZED AREA OF MIAMI INTO A VIBRANT COMMUNITY DEDICATED TO ART AND DESIGN

The Miami Design District is home to art galleries, design showrooms, artist lofts, design and architecture firms, media companies, luxury retail, restaurants and urban residences, as well as internationally renowned cultural events. The neighborhood is continuing to be transformed into a vibrant new destination where the branded urban elements are a critical component of the visitor's experience.

FROM SCULPTURES AND ARCHITECTURAL FACADES, TO STOREFRONTS AND HANDPAINTED MURALS, THE DISTRICT HAS CURATED AN ATYPICAL, HIGHLY CREATIVE RETAIL DESTINATION EXPERIENCE THAT DRAWS WORLD-CLASS TENANTS AND VISITORS FROM AROUND THE WORLD

THE ROLE OF PUBLIC ART IN THE MIAMI DESIGN DISTRICT IS TO ADD A DYNAMIC LAYER OF CHARACTER TO THE AREA, AS WELL AS AID IN NAVIGATION AND A VISITOR'S SENSE OF PLACE WITHIN THE PROJECT

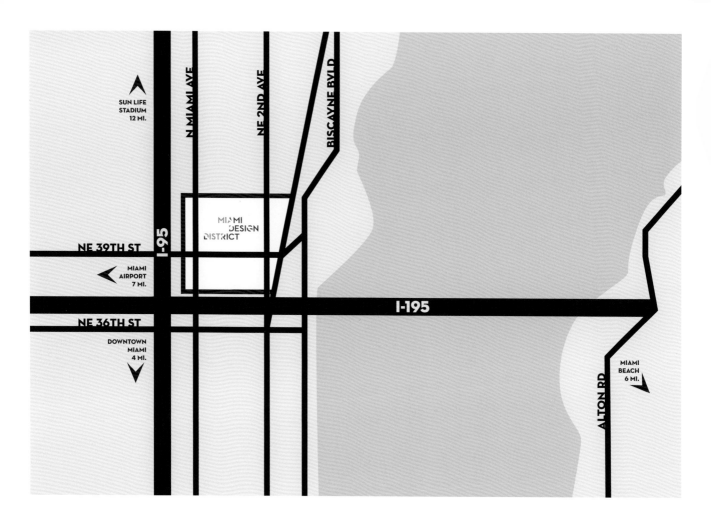

"HERE WAS OUR OPPORTUNITY TO HELP DEFINE MIAMI AS A CULTURAL DESTINATION BY CREATING A NEIGHBORHOOD THAT ADVOCATES CREATIVITY THROUGH DESIGN, ART, FOOD AND FASHION…"

— CRAIG ROBBINS, CEO, DACRA

In the early history of the property, the plot of land that was to become the Miami Design District was a pineapple farm. It changed hands and owners throughout time, and in the 70's and 80's, the Design District was a blossoming wholesale furniture and design center. However, the area declined in popularity as newer design centers formed around the city, and it began decaying into a gritty and underutilized neighborhood of Miami.

Craig Robins (Dacra) had begun buying buildings in the area over two decades ago with plans to revitalize the 9 block district into a luxury shopping destination, and finally, after a year of discussion, in 2010, a partnership was inked with Michael Burke (Louis Vuitton Worldwide), Bernard Arnault (LVMH), and L Real Estate.

Many luxury brands were eager to get a foothold in the new district and couldn't pass the opportunity to open 10-20,000 sq ft flagships in the new Miami Design District. As Marshal Cohen of the NDP Groups says, "[The Miami Design District is] about the brand being able to showcase the lifestyle of the brand, rather than a selected version of pieces of the brand."

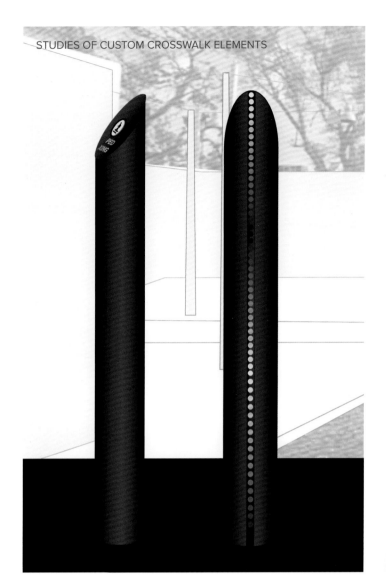

THE TEAM WORKED WITH AN INTERNATIONAL GROUP OF ARCHITECTS AND CONSULTANTS TO CURATE A SERIES OF UNIQUE URBAN ELEMENTS THAT ARE A CRITICAL COMPONENT OF THE VISITOR EXPERIENCE

Atypical applications were created for the environmental graphics in the district including urban maps, civic wayfinding elements, custom crosswalks, parking wayfinding, and didactic signs for the art collection dispersed throughout the area. The challenge in the project was to design signage that was aptly informative and clear, but also elegant and sophisticated enough to stand next to some of the highest-end retailers in the world. There was a special emphasis on highlighting the artful moments strategically placed throughout, and in places, the signage takes a museum-like approach, providing just enough information to allow visitors to focus on the art and retailers.

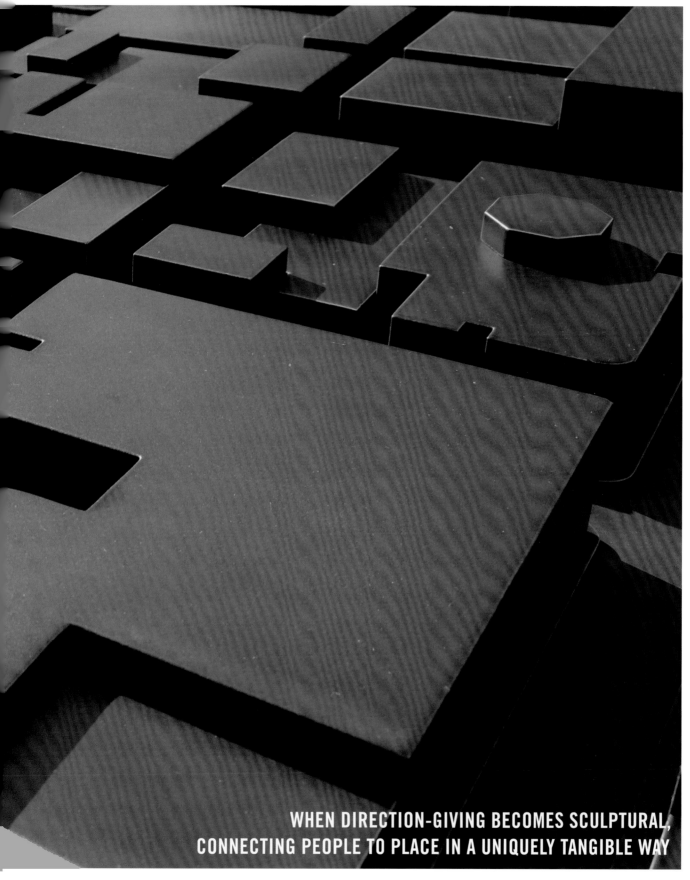

WHEN DIRECTION-GIVING BECOMES SCULPTURAL,
CONNECTING PEOPLE TO PLACE IN A UNIQUELY TANGIBLE WAY

"...THIS LITTLE MODEL OF THE MIAMI DESIGN DISTRICT... MAY BE THE SLEEKEST, DARE WE SAY COOLEST, MALL GUIDE MAP EVER."

— SEAN MCCAUGHAN, CURBED - MIAMI

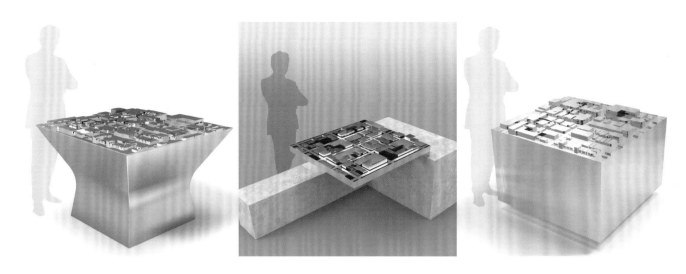

AS A STUDY ON URBAN DIRECTORIES, THE TEAM SOUGHT NEW WAYS
TO CONNECT PEOPLE TO A PLACE, BUT THROUGH AN ARTFUL LEAP

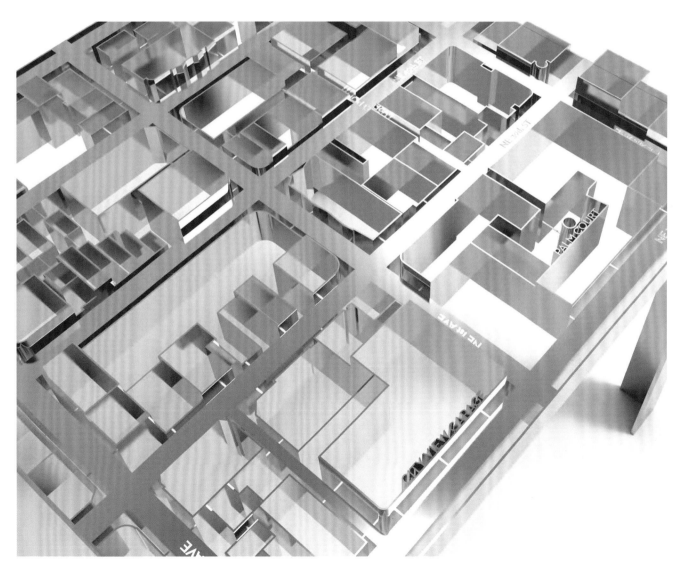

"IF NEIGHBORHOODS WERE TECH COMPANIES, THE DESIGN DISTRICT MIGHT BE APPLE, BECAUSE THE ATTENTION TO AESTHETICS IS PROVING INCREDIBLY ALL-ENCOMPASSING."

— SEAN MCCAUGHAN, CURBED - MIAMI

NETSCAPE (2010/2014)
BY KONSTANTIN GRCIC

Netscape is a 21-seat web of hanging chairs by celebrated German designer Konstantin Grcic. The interactive work consists of a six-point star-shaped modular frame, from which seats made of fiberglass and polypropylene netting are suspended to form a series of hammock-like swings that rock gently when used by visitors.

55

EXIT.

THE DISTRICT
Abu Dhabi, United Arab Emirates

THE DISTRICT

ABU DHABI, UNITED ARAB EMIRATES

THE DISTRICT IS COMPRISED OF LUXURY FLAGSHIPS, DESTINATION DINING, GOURMET ÉPICERIE, LIFESTYLE SERVICES, CINEMAS, DESIGN SHOWROOMS, AND INTERNATIONAL GALLERIES

The Arabian Gulf's distinct indoor-outdoor retail neighborhood offers a unique shopping environment integrating "High Street" experience with mall convenience and service. The District's unique Luxury Street, High Street and Crescent Arcade retail environments will comprise the largest collection of brands assembled in one location in Abu Dhabi. The team—comprised of designers and creative problem solvers— brings years of urban and mixed-use retail signage and graphics expertise to this unique and vibrant metropolitan environment that is being created. Strategically surrounded by three world-class museums—the Louvre Abu Dhabi, Zayed National Museum, and Guggenheim Abu Dhabi— the design team's sensibilities helped create the type of destination worthy of a highly visible and unparalleled retail and lifestyle experience.

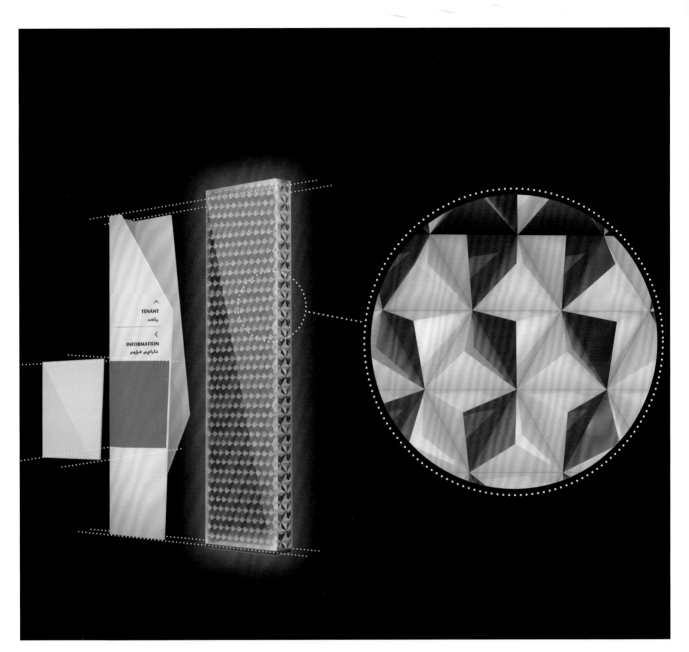

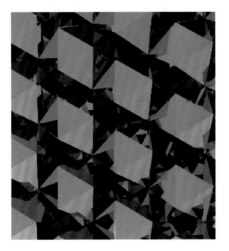

LUXURY STREET

↑

Zayed
National
Museum
مركز الفنون التمثيلية

→

Louvre Abu Dhabi
مركز الفنون التمثيلية

LUXURY
STREET

THE DISTRICT

1 PARK PLAZA

IRVINE COMPANY

OFFICE PROPERTIES

MULTIPLE LOCATIONS

THE CREATION OF A COMPREHENSIVE ICONOGRAPHY, WAYFINDING SYSTEM, AND MAP GUIDELINES TO HELP IMPLEMENT NEW CUSTOMER OFFERINGS IN THE WORKPLACE

Irvine Company Office Properties (ICOP) was rolling out an amenity initiative across 150 locations nationwide intended to enhance the customer experience. Already in place were numerous amenities, such as dry cleaning pick-up and convenience stores, but relatively few customers knew they existed. Additionally, ICOP was implementing some new "premium" amenities intended to provide spaces to gather and recharge. State-of-the-art fitness and wellness centers ("Kinetic"), outdoor workspaces, Wi-Fi, BBQ, and Bocce ("Commons") were amongst the additions intended to enhance the work-life balance. With all of these offerings, ICOP was in need of a standard visual language.

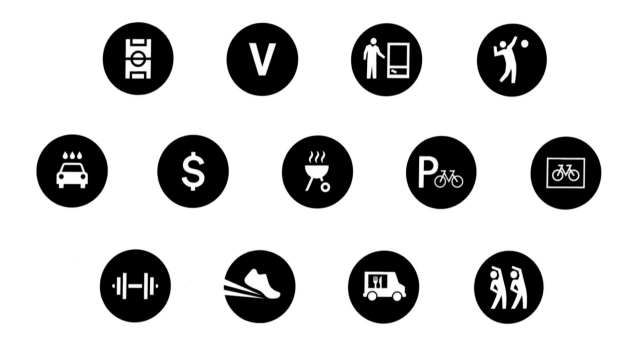

STARFIELD HANAM
Hanam, South Korea

FORUM
CUERNAVACA

FORUM CUERNAVACA

CUERNAVACA, MEXICO

THE SITE OF FORUM CUERNAVACA WASN'T ALWAYS THE VIBRANT AND ENGAGING SHOPPING CENTER IT IS NOW

In recent history it was the site of a massive sewing factory, and when the developer, GICSA, purchased the property, it was important that they preserve the structure of the original factory. What was needed was a redeveloped brand, as well as a system of graphics and wayfinding for the site. The overall design was driven by the complex site plan and need for navigation. Sign locations and messaging were top concerns in the process. The team started by designating a system of colors and patterns to allow guests to create a clear mental map of the project. The repurposed water tower served a landmark for both vehicular and pedestrian visitors. Inspiration came from the textiles embedded in the site's history and the cut-out detail in the signage design connected the past to the present. Additionally, taking queues from the existing site, hundreds of sewing machines were repurposed into art installations throughout the center.

↑ FERIA
↑ FOOD HALL
↑ CINES
← PLAZA PRINCIPAL
← MOTOR LOBBY

↑ 🚹 🚺

THE STAR: HOME OF THE DALLAS COWBOYS
Frisco, Texas

HOME OF THE DALLAS COWBOYS
THE STAR

FRISCO, TEXAS

THE STAR IS A 91-ACRE PREMIER SPORTS AND ENTERTAINMENT DISTRICT IN FRISCO, TEXAS THAT IS HOME TO THE WORLD FAMOUS DALLAS COWBOYS

About 25 miles north of Dallas, The Star features a hotel, shopping and entertainment venues, offices, a sports medicine center, two outdoor practice fields, and a 12,000-seat indoor stadium. The heart of the project was to create an experience that celebrated and honored both the players and fans of the Dallas Cowboys franchise. Building on the iconic blue star logo, a memorable and navigable exterior wayfinding and signage system was created. The sign family included large scale pylons and digital integration, enhancing an exciting environment worthy of "America's Football Team."

ALI'I

KA MAKANA ALI'I
Kapolei, Hawaii

KA MAKANA ALI'I

KAPOLEI, HAWAII

INSPIRED BY THE NATIVE FLORA OF THIS GROWING COMMUNITY WEST OF HONOLULU

DeBartolo and the Department of Hawaiian Homelands, built a combined lifestyle and power center with a local Hawaiian flavor. The bright colors, dynamic angles, and internal illumination utilized throughout the site helped to bring a fun and spirited character. The signage and wayfinding program has since become a vibrant addition, expressing the brand story in a bold and memorable way.

THE NAME KA MAKANA ALI'I TRANSLATES TO "THE ROYAL GIFT"
AND IS A TRIBUTE TO PRINCE JONAH KUHIO KALANIANA'OLE,
WHO HELPED DESIGNATE HUNDREDS OF THOUSANDS OF ACRES
OF GOVERNMENT LAND IN HAWAII TO NATIVE HAWAIIANS

The idea of a gift, traditionally wrapped in a Ti Leaf, became the primary inspiration for the design. The rich brand story became the backbone across the signage and wayfinding design program. Additionally, drawing a pattern based on the colors and folding of the Ti Leaf became iconic throughout the project. As you travel from the perimeter of the mall toward the interior, the color story moves from teal to fuschia, representing this surprise or unfolding of the dynamic gift.

MACY'S ↑
FOREVER 21 ↑
FOOD ↑
MARKET
ʻŌLINO ↑
THEATRES
H&M ↑

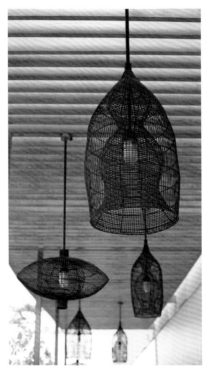

ʻŌLINO ↑
THEATRES
HAMPTON INN ↑
& SUITES
MACY'S →
H&M →

The circulation of a power center and a lifestyle center vary dramatically from one another. The environmental graphic design program created, bridged that gap and promoted a cohesive feeling with strong pedestrian connections between the far reaches of the parking lots into the heart of the shopping center.

THINK

MENTAL CONNECTION TO A PLACE THROUGH STORYTELLING ELEMENTS THAT REFERENCE HISTORY AND A CULTURAL SENSE OF PLACE

When working in university, workplace, and city center projects, it is important to focus on the unique opportunities related to user groups, scale and connectivity. Scale and function of environments paired with the complexity of individual user needs and expectations provide breadth and depth to the design approach. Creating connections between destinations by paths of travel, decision-points or meeting places within the project translate into design opportunities to meet the challenges of creating interconnectivity.

Designers work to create elements that encourage people to connect to the places where they gather. The psychology behind spaces of congregation is an important factor in helping to understand their function and form and to ensure active links are created to connect these spaces. Links are achieved through wayfinding, landmarks, placemaking elements and brand touchpoints to reinforce an intuitive sense of place.

It is true that building connections has the larger benefit of adding to the life of a community. Creating a sense of belonging, pride and ownership are powerful goals for the success of an interconnected campus. The ultimate result is the mingling of ideas, cultures, philosophies and values that support the overall vision.

CASE STUDY

UNIVERSITY OF CALIFORNIA
RIVERSIDE

RIVERSIDE, CALIFORNIA

CONNECTING THE CAMPUS COMMUNITY THROUGH THOUGHTFUL PLACEMAKING STRATEGIES

Work took place alongside the students and development team to develop placemaking strategies that connect the community to the UC Riverside campus. Wayfinding design, environmental graphics, and branding were integral elements that enhanced connectivity on campus and a greater sense of place. The overall goal was to create an innovative and exciting atmosphere for the UC Riverside students, faculty and staff.

MAKING CAMPUS CONNECTIONS

THE HUB IS THE PRIMARY GATHERING PLACE FOR THE CAMPUS COMMUNITY TO EAT, RELAX, MEET AND COLLABORATE

The HUB (Highlander Union Building) is the central destination where the UCR community gathers. The space provides dining and retail facilities, meeting areas, lounges and event spaces. The HUB is also the seat of the student government, student organizations and student affairs. This core community center was enhanced through environmental graphic elements to facilitate activity and movement through clear wayfinding and placemaking strategies.

PLACEMAKING ELEMENTS BECOME FAMILIAR AND ICONIC LANDMARKS ON THE CAMPUS LANDSCAPE, PROVIDING ORIENTATION AND BUILDING AN INTUITIVE SENSE OF PLACE

THE UCR MONUMENT HAS BECOME A BELOVED LANDMARK ON CAMPUS
AS THE BACKDROP OF COUNTLESS PHOTOGRAPHS THAT MARK SIGNIFICANT
AND MEMORABLE MOMENTS IN THE UNIVERSITY'S HISTORY

OLD PARKLAND
Dallas, Texas

THE FINAL GUIDELINES FORMALIZED THE PLAN FOR IMPLEMENTING THESE
THEMES INTO THE SITE, UTILIZING EVERYTHING FROM QUOTES, HISTORICAL
MOTIFS, PAVING GRAPHICS, REFLECTION POOLS AND BRONZE STATUES

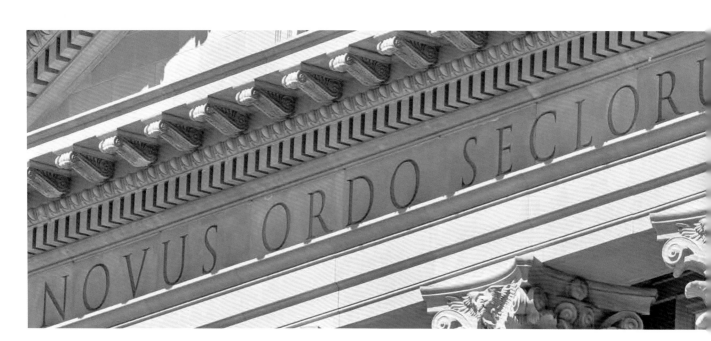

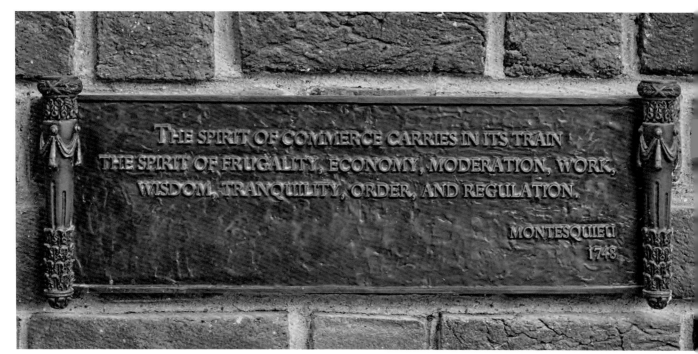

C'EST UNE
EXPÉRIENCE
ÉTERNELLE QUE
TOUT HOMME QUI
A DU POUVOIR EST
PORTÉ À EN ABUSER
IL VA JUSQU'À CE
QU'IL TROUVE
DES LIMITES.

POUR QU'ON
NE PUISSE ABUSER
DU POUVOIR, IL
FAUT QUE, PAR LA
DISPOSITION DES
CHOSES, LE POUVOIR
ARRÊTE LE POUVOIR.

MONTESQUIEU
1748

" BUT CONSTANT EXPERIENCE
SHOWS US THAT EVERY MAN
INVESTED WITH POWER IS
APT TO ABUSE IT, AND TO
CARRY HIS AUTHORITY AS
FAR AS IT WILL GO. IS IT NOT
STRANGE, THOUGH TRUE,
TO SAY THAT VIRTUE ITSELF
HAS NEED OF LIMITS?

TO PREVENT THIS ABUSE,
IT IS NECESSARY FROM THE
VERY NATURE OF THINGS
THAT POWER SHOULD BE
A CHECK TO POWER."

— MONTESQUIEU, 1748

↗

2 & 3

DUGONI SCHOOL OF DENTISTRY
San Francisco, California

STAYING TRUE TO THE SCHOOL'S INNOVATIVE STYLE AND VISION

It was an intentional decision for the design to reflect the university's cutting edge technology. Powerful graphics clearly communicate to a wide range of consumers including those who speak differing languages. It is the acute attention to detail within the practice of dentistry that was taken into account when addressing all facets of the project. Additionally, the high-end facility and impressive state-of-the-art technology were funded by groups of generous donors, adding on another aspect to the site's environmental graphic design: donor recognition.

HUTTO
PATTERSON
PEDIATRIC
CLINIC

999 THIRD AVENUE
Seattle, Washington

WELLS FARGO CENTER
999 THIRD AVENUE

SEATTLE, WASHINGTON

REVITALIZING THE WELLS FARGO CENTER AT 999 THIRD AVENUE

The new owners of the building, which is a 47 story building from the 1980's, aimed to reposition the lobbies to help attract a wider variety of tenants. Alongside JLL Commercial Real Estate and Mithun, the design plan was to develop a branding and logo system, create a holistic identity, and refresh of the exterior as well as the interior lobby to give it a modern and timeless look.

The objectives were clear from the beginning—to activate and simplify the public space. Using simple and legible signage, the team was able to create a modern and timeless setting for work and gathering. The new lighting alongside the updated signage solutions helped attract passers-by from the street, and all parts of the interior design help reinforce the connection to the building's greater context.

THE BUDDY HOLLY HALL OF PERFORMING ARTS AND SCIENCES
Lubbock, Texas

THE BUDDY HOLLY HALL

OF PERFORMING ARTS AND SCIENCES

LUBBOCK, TEXAS

THE BUDDY HOLLY HALL OF PERFORMING ARTS AND SCIENCES IS A SPACE DEDICATED TO MUSIC AND VISUAL ARTS

The center stands to honor the late Buddy Holly and the music he created, as well as the music of Lubbock and Western Texas overall. It will become the cultural hub of Lubbock and the cornerstone of the downtown revitalization, as well as the homes of Ballet Lubbock, Lubbock Symphony Orchestra, and Lubbock ISD Visual and Performing Arts. With a campus size of over 220,000 square feet, a developed system of signage and wayfinding to guide visitors to the various theaters and practice areas was implemented around the space.

A PROJECT OF THIS SCALE AND CALIBER WOULD NOT BE POSSIBLE WITHOUT THE DONATIONS OF COMMUNITY MEMBERS AND STAKEHOLDERS

In order to recognize these vital parties, the design team was tasked to create a comprehensive donor recognition program, in addition to the wayfinding and identity signage. The program includes opportunities throughout the site for the names of donors to be celebrated. The most iconic display is a pick wall, incorporating thousands of guitar picks of various sizes creating an image of Buddy Holly's iconic Fender guitar. This piece is visible through the front windows of the building and is the primary focal point for visitors as they approach the site.

PIZZA HUT CORPORATE HEADQUARTERS
Dallas, Texas

UC IRVINE, MESA COURT TOWERS
Irvine, California

THE ANTEATERY
FITNESS/REC CTR
MAIL SERVICES
THE COURT
CONEJO SUITE
HOUSING OFFICE
COMMUNITY CTR

UNIVERSITY OF CALIFORNIA, IRVINE

MESA COURT TOWERS

IRVINE, CALIFORNIA

FOR THE FIRST TIME IN 30 YEARS, THE UNIVERSITY OF CALIFORNIA, IRVINE MADE A MASSIVE EXPANSION TO THEIR ON-CAMPUS RESIDENTIAL BUILDINGS

The Mesa Court towers are three 6-story halls designed to house over 900 students, and include a dining hall, a student services center, mail center, and a computer lounge. The design work was centered around interior and exterior signage and environmental graphics for the new student housing buildings, as well as monument signage, pedestrian wayfinding directories, a series of blade signs for amenities, and public art pieces at the entrance of each hall. Naming and branding efforts for The Anteatery, a dining hall, were also included.

IN THE UNIVERSITY MARKET, THE CURRENT COMPETITION FOCUSES JUST AS MUCH ON AMENITY OFFERING AND STUDENT LIFE AS IT DOES ON ACADEMICS

In the University market, the current competition focuses just as much on amenity offering and student life as it does on academics. The challenge at hand was to provide creative design solutions that meet the rising expectations of today's students. A family of signage was created using three main design elements: a deep, espresso brown cabinet structure, metal slats that echo the architecture from Mithun, and a concrete base. Carrying these motifs throughout, an innovative design solution was created that met the client's modest budget. Additionally, the design team produced a series of mural graphics at the entrance of each hall and the Anteatery, which added to the character and value of the spaces.

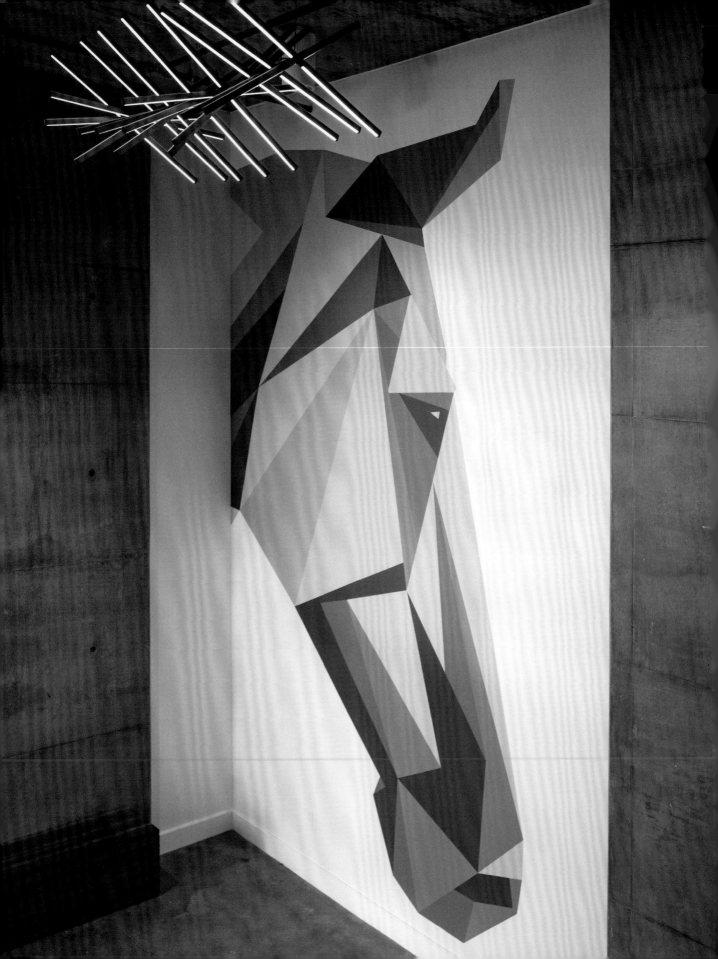

TOWN SQUARE DUBAI

Dubai, United Arab Emirates

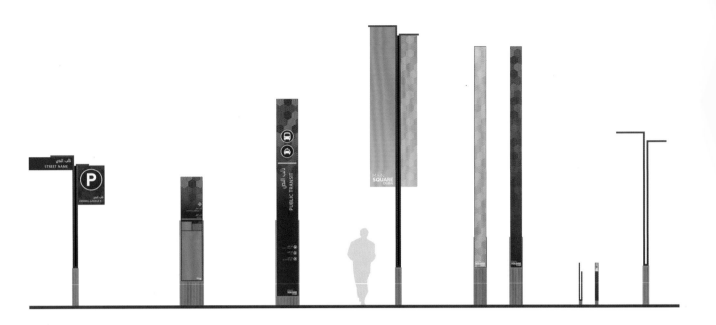

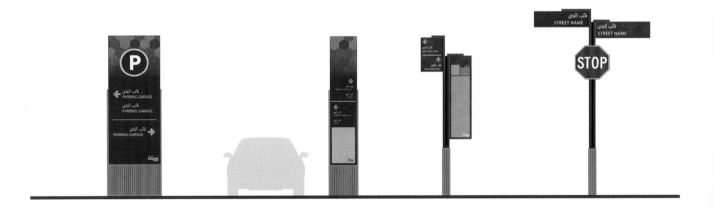

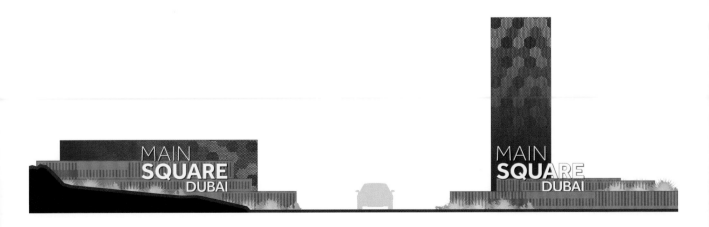

ACTIVATE

PHYSICAL CONNECTION TO A PLACE, THROUGH MOVEMENT AND SPATIAL CHARACERISTICS EXPERIENCED THROUGH THE SENSES

The ultimate goal when working in the built environment is to connect people to place. Monuments and directional signs are important environmental tools that provide the cues for arrival at a location and successful navigation of a project, adding comfort and confidence for visitors. Referencing Kevin Lynch's book "The Image of the City," these signs serve as tools that empower people to create a clear mental map of a place utilizing the elements of paths, edges, districts, nodes and landmarks. Resulting is a highly functional approach to wayfinding that helps connect people to place, and ultimately, optimal activation of a place.

When working on a project, designers should keep in mind connecting people to place— to get people to actively experience the entire project. When guests arrive at a destination they should explore and be delighted and stimulated. Activating and connecting people to environments also includes branded elements such as logos and environmental graphics, which add layers to enrich the overall experience. These layers create connections to a place through overarching impressions of a project, as well as through placemaking details which create memorable moments with a place, building long-term connections and return visits.

CASE STUDY

THE SUMMIT BECHTEL RESERVE

BOY SCOUTS OF AMERICA

MT. HOPE, WEST VIRGINIA

MAXIMIZING THE UNIQUE PHYSICAL CONNECTION OF PEOPLE TO PLACE TO EMBODY THE SCOUT EXPERIENCE ON 10,000 ACRES IN WEST VIRGINIA

Located in Mt. Hope, West Virginia, the large-scale outdoor facility was designed for the Boy Scouts of America. The overall scope of the project included branding and sign programs for the site's different components. The three components included The Summit at Bechtel Reserve, Base Camp Charlie and the graphic elements for the 2013 and 2017 National Jamborees, along with the 2019 World Scout Jamboree. The project challenge was to develop a coordinated and adaptable approach to connecting the Boy Scouts to this vast site. The physical connection of people to place was a key feature for each step, keeping in mind the multisensory experiences of the programs that would be hosted at the site.

TIMELINE

The team fostered a long-term relationship with the Boy Scouts of America to develop the permanent and temporary branding, placemaking and wayfinding for the Summit and the National Scout Jamboree events. The involvement in the planning of this site began with the strategies defined in the Source Book in 2008, laying the groundwork for the design principles that would guide future decisions and development.

2008

DESIGN CHARETTE
10-day design charette in West Virginia to produce overall strategy for Summit Bechtel Reserve

2010

DESIGN BEGINS
Simultaneous design work begins for the permanent sign elements for Summit Bechtel Reserve and the 2013 National Scout Jamboree

2012

DESIGN IMPLEMENTATION

2013

THE SUMMIT OPENS

2013 NATIONAL SCOUT JAMBOREE

2014–17

DESIGN BEGINS
Design for the 2017 National Scout Jamboree

DESIGN IMPLEMENTATION

2017

2017 NATIONAL SCOUT JAMBOREE

2018

PLANNING
Plans for the 2019 World Scout Jamboree begin

2019

2019 WORLD SCOUT JAMBOREE

SBR

THE FIRST STEPS WERE TO DEVELOP A LOGO AND BRAND FOR BOTH THE SUMMIT AND THE NATIONAL JAMBOREE. THE BRAND THOUGHTFULLY INCORPORATED A SENSE OF PLACE THAT WOULD HELP CONNECT THE BOY SCOUTS OF AMERICA TO THE PHYSICAL CHARACTER OF BECHTEL RESERVE.

The scale of the project both in size of the site as well as the number of stakeholders and consultants involved was a challenge that required great coordination and a clear process. The placemaking components were carefully designed, taking into consideration site grading nuances, infrastructure requirements and environmentally-conscious design principles.

There was careful attention to every aspect of The Summit Bechtel Reserve, including overall identity and wayfinding, camping areas, basecamp activity areas, and The Summit Center. Balancing the aesthetic between the natural sense of place the site brings with the contemporary attitudes of the activities and innovative areas that are being created. This project was the winner of the SEGD Honor award in the leisure/entertainment environment category.

BASE CAMP CHARLIE WAS A TEST RUN UTILIZING A COLOR-CODED VILLAGE
SYSTEM THAT WOULD EVENTUALLY BE BUILT THROUGHOUT THE 10,000 ACRE
SITE FOR THE NATIONAL JAMBOREES

THE PROGRAM RESPONDED TO THE NATURAL CONTEXT OF THE SITE AS WELL AS THE CRAFTED QUALITIES OF LOCAL MATERIALS, MIXED WITH THE CONTEMPORARY ATTITUDES OF THE ADVENTURE ACTIVITIES TO CREATE UNIQUE JUXTAPOSITIONS WITHIN THE SITE SIGNS. DESIGNS QUICKLY MOVED FROM CONCEPT TO DESIGN INTENT, THEN EXPERTLY BROUGHT TO LIFE.

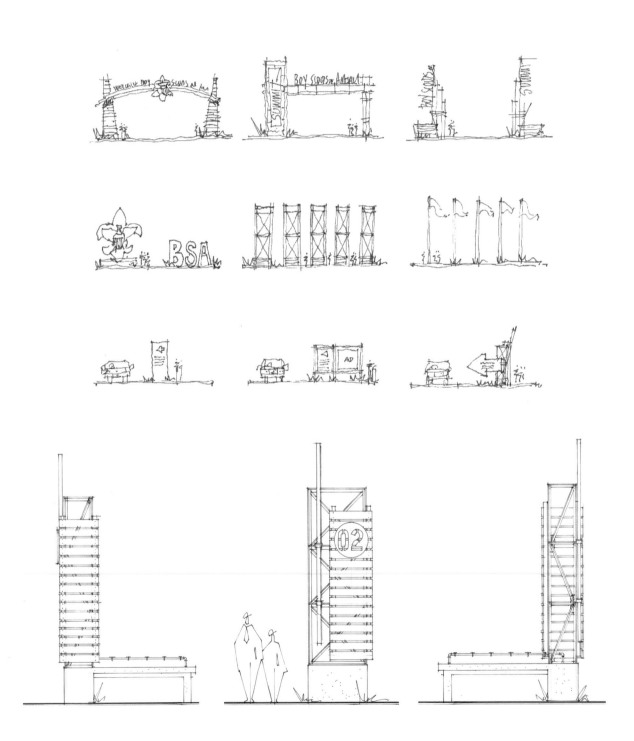

NAMES WERE GIVEN TO EACH OF THE ACTIVITIES, DISTRICTS AND ATTRACTIONS, THEN A CRAFTED IDENTITY AND THE APPROPRIATE ENVIRONMENTAL GRAPHIC ELEMENTS. SIGN COMPONENTS WERE DESIGNED TO BE INEXPENSIVE AND FLEXIBLE WITH NO EXTRANEOUS MATERIAL USAGE OR SUPERFLUOUS DETAILING.

LOCATED ON A 10,000-ACRE SITE ADJACENT TO THE NEW RIVER GORGE NATIONAL PARK AREA, THE SUMMIT IS A UNIQUE HIGH-ADVENTURE CAMP

2013 NATIONAL JAMBOREE

The 2013 National Jamboree was the first event held at the Summit Bechtel Reserve in West Virginia, the new home for the Boy Scouts of America's camps and jamborees. This was the 18th National Scout Jamboree held by the organization. The event hosted approximately 70,000 Boy Scouts, Venturer Scouts, Volunteers and SBR Staff for a 10-day extravaganza of adventure sports, merit badge exchanging, concerts, and scout honor. This jamboree was operated similarly to a World Scout Jamboree with sub camps that promoted maximum interaction.

LIVE
SCOUTING'S
ADVENTURE
2017 NATIONAL JAMBOREE

2019 WORLD SCOUT JAMBOREE

WEST END & THE POOLS
LAS PISCINAS Y EL WEST END
LES PISCINES ET LE EST END

LIVING IN THE 21st CENTURY
World Scout Jamboree 2019

KNOWLEDGE WORKFORCE
CONOCIMIENTO DE LA FUERZA LABORAL
CONNAISSANCE DE MAIN-D'ŒUVRE

FUTURE OF TRANSPORTATION
FUTURO DEL TRANSPORTE
L'AVENIR DES TRANSPORTS

MORE THAN 40,000 SCOUTS FROM 152 COUNTRIES ATTENDED

SUMMIT CENTER

ASBURY PARK WATERFRONT
Asbury Park, New Jersey

ASBURY PARK WATERFRONT

ASBURY PARK, NEW JERSEY

IT HAS BEEN SAID THAT ASBURY PARK IS THE BIGGEST LITTLE CITY BY THE SEA

In the past, Asbury Park was known as a music, entertainment, and international coastal destination, where the sheer innovation and fierce creativity was an attraction in and of itself. Today the city's tradition of creativity is alive and well, taking shape in various art forms ranging from sculpture, music, street art, and murals. Inspired by the creativity, eclecticism, culture, and hand crafted quality of its architecture, the team worked to develop a signage system that seeks to identify, connect and enhance the experience that is Asbury Park.

Asbury Park, N. J.

PLAZA

Swan Ride on Wesley
and Asbury Par

CAROUSEL

Boardwalk and Casino, Asbury Park, N. J.

4th Ave. Beach Scene, Showing Convention Hall, Asbury Park, N. J.

CONVENTION HALL AND 7th AVENUE PAVILION, ASBURY P

Ave. at Press Plaza, Asbury Par

LIGGETT'S

GREETINGS from

ASBURY PARK

N. J.

AN ECLECTIC COMMUNITY OF MAKERS AND DOERS, ENTREPRENEURS AND INNOVATORS, ARTISTS AND VISIONARIES...

...as well as a city in transition, Asbury Park embraces its past, both the good and the bad, providing a sense of authenticity, uniqueness, and grit that cannot be replicated. It's a culture that celebrates quirkiness, honors originality, and radiates creativity. Focusing on quality products, services, and experiences, the local restaurateurs, creatives, and residents have helped breathe new life into the spirit of Asbury Park. The energy and optimism about the future is contagious and the dream of greatness is quickly becoming a reality.

PEOPLE OF ALL AGES, GENDERS, ETHNICITIES, AND CULTURES FIND A COMMONALITY IN THEIR LOVE FOR THIS SPECIAL PLACE.

RESTAURATEUR

IT IS A GREAT CANVAS FOR CREATING AND INSPIRING.

PLANNING CONSULTANT

I LOVE THAT I CAN GO FOR A SWIM IN THE OCEAN AFTER WORK, EAT KOREAN FUSION TACOS ON THE BOARDWALK, AND LISTEN TO A REALLY GREAT BAND PLAY LIVE MUSIC EVERY NIGHT OF THE WEEK.

SECOND HAND BIKES

ASBURY PARK IS THE BIGGEST, NOT SO LITTLE CITY ON THE SHORE.

SUMMERTIME SURF

WHAT PEOPLE ARE SAYING

IT IS THE PEOPLE OF ASBURY PARK THAT MAKE IT GREAT, IT'S THE DIVERSITY THAT MAKES IT UNIQUE, AND IT'S THE CREATIVE SPIRIT OF INNOVATION AND TRANSFORMATION THAT HAS MADE IT FAMOUS.

ARTIST / DEVELOPER

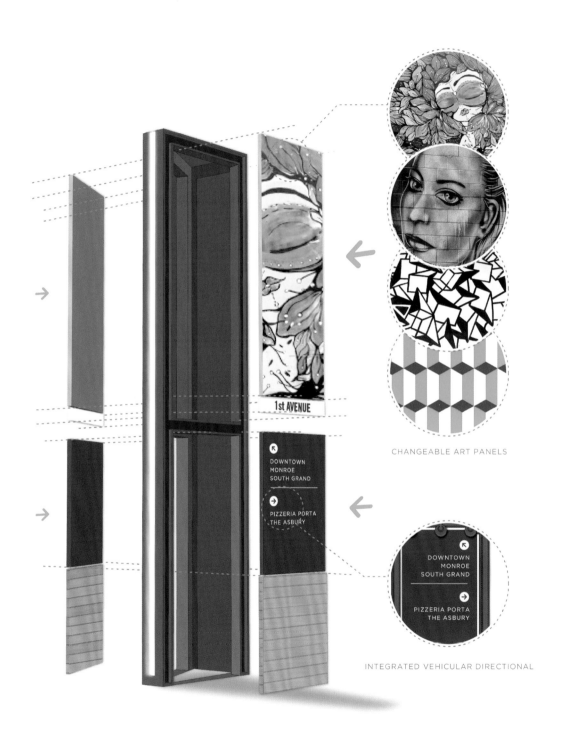

1st AVENUE

DOWNTOWN
MONROE
SOUTH GRAND

PIZZERIA PORTA
THE ASBURY

CHANGEABLE ART PANELS

DOWNTOWN
MONROE
SOUTH GRAND

PIZZERIA PORTA
THE ASBURY

INTEGRATED VEHICULAR DIRECTIONAL

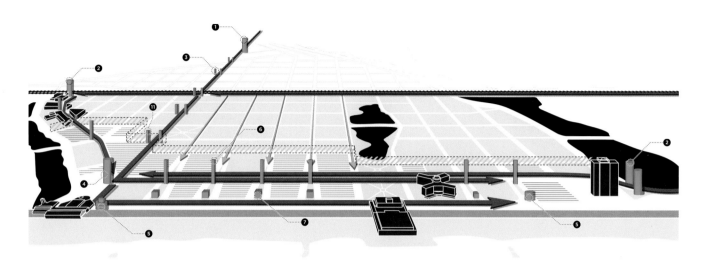

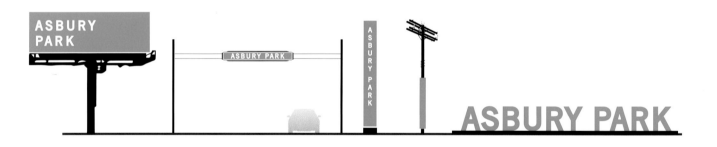

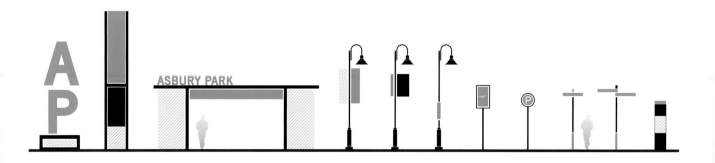

CREATING AN URBAN EDGE
FLEXIBLE PAVILIONS

The success of Ocean Avenue relies heavily on the development of a strong pedestrian connection across the street, activating the spaces in between, and giving the user cause to explore. The proposed design for the flexible pavilions located along Ocean Avenue uses a simple steel support frame that can be broken up into three individual sections to allow for multiple uses—retail tenants and cafes that transform into vibrant active spaces during operation hours, bike storage and amenity rentals for guests and visitors, even open air pavilions with seating, restrooms, and lockers. There is also an opportunity to integrate the street name into the pavilions, branding them as 'Second Avenue Pavilion,' etc. to reference the similar technique used on the boardwalk.

GREAT PARK NEIGHBORHOODS

Irvine, California

ORANGE COUNTY

GREAT PARK NEIGHBORHOODS

IRVINE, CALIFORNIA

THE IRVINE GREAT PARK IS ICONIC TO THE REGION AND ONE OF A KIND IN SIZE AND FEATURES

The park is a collection of unique neighborhoods and amenities joined together by immense walking and biking trails—eventually linking to the Irvine Transportation Center. Working closely with FivePoint Communities, the team created signage and wayfinding for each neighborhood as well as a unifying master plan signage system that creates and encourages visitors to engage in all that the park has to offer.

SURROUNDING THE GREAT PARK IS A SERIES OF NEW NEIGHBORHOODS, EACH WITH THEIR OWN NAME, PARK, AND CHARACTER

Complete with miles of walking and biking trails, each neighborhood offers convenient access to the Great Park and all the amenities Irvine has to offer, including some of the top-ranking schools in the state. The intention behind the environmental graphic design was to help each neighborhood a distinct personality, through signage and wayfinding graphics.

PAVILION PARK

Pavilion Park is the first of several communities developed by Great Park Neighborhoods, sited around the perimeter of the Orange County Great Park. Though a brand new development, Pavilion Park aims to mix contemporary design with the character of the area, adding historic relevance to the site by featuring an artful blend of graphics and signage.

THE PATIO

SPORTS COURT

NGE BALLOON

PAVILION PARK

PLAYGROUND

POOL & SPA

LOOKOUT

BEACON PARK

Beacon Park is the second of several communities developed by Great Park Neighborhoods. The team worked closely with 5 Point Communities to create signage and wayfinding that stood out, giving Beacon Park its own identity within the Great Park Neighborhood system. The design was inspired by clarifying the navigation and incorporating a mid-century modern design to create a palette that pops.

PARASOL PARK

The Parasol Park development focuses on a higher density of housing, and features a large community park, garden, greenhouse, and community building. The Great Park Neighborhoods partnered with The Ecology Center to create a natural space to gather as a community and will also facilitate weekly and monthly family activities. Parasol Park is the third development in the Great Park Neighborhoods community, and will become a social center for the families who move in.

A SYSTEM OF PARK SIGNAGE AND WAYFINDING, SPECIALTY AND TEMPORARY GRAPHICS, AND GARDEN SIGNAGE ALONGSIDE THE ECOLOGY CENTER

The team was inspired to create a look and feel for the neighborhood that was hand crafted and high quality. Wood and handpainted identity elements were carried throughout, and many signs featured hand drawn and playful typography and illustrations. Elements from The Ecology Center brand were carried into the garden signage, which created a sense of unity and cohesiveness across the two brands. The end result was a highly integrated system of signage and wayfinding that helped bring the garden and community spaces to life.

CADENCE PARK

Cadence Park is another dynamic connecting park within the Great Park Neighborhoods in Irvine, California. It is an artfully curated community park with areas of rest, engaging installations, and buildings designed for performing and community arts. The signage and wayfinding elements are modern yet have a playful quality to them. Pops of color and polished surfaces reflect the surroundings and create movement as you navigate through the park. Unique building identities and signage were created to give the guests a clear and fun way to differentiate the buildings. Additionally, murals create moments of placemaking in between the public spaces.

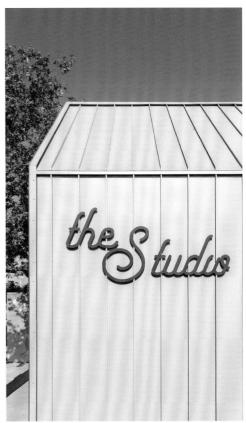

THE POOLS

An 8-acre park inside of the Great Park Neighborhoods in Irvine, California, The Pools is the newest offering for residents of the neighborhoods. Consisting of a junior Olympic-sized pool, a family pool, a children's pool, three spas, as well as sand volleyball courts, a clubhouse, and general fitness areas, this park truly emcompasses the spirit of the outdoors. The entire team collaborated to develop high end and welcoming identity signage and regulatory signage, and helped curate a series of artful moments meant to inspire and amaze guests and residents.

OAKBROOK CENTER
Oakbrook, Illinois

OAKBROOK CENTER

OAKBROOK, ILLINOIS

THE OAKBROOK CENTER, LOCATED IN THE WESTERN CHICAGO SUBURBS, IS A MIXED-USE DESTINATION FEATURING A COLLECTION OF BOUTIQUE RETAILERS, DINING, HOSPITALITY, AND ENTERTAINMENT OFFERINGS

The team worked closely with the team to update the previously dated center, creating an elegant character by envisioning an atmosphere that is classic and timeless, yet modern and engaging. The creative placemaking design incorporates a large common space to accommodate events and create a sense of community. The design package included a new brand, identity, and wayfinding signage system that complemented the fashionable environment with a bold use of black complemented by a striking color, bringing a fresh new look to the center.

FIRST AND BROADWAY PARK
Los Angeles, California

FAB PARK

LOS ANGELES, CALIFORNIA

FAB PARK IS A LANDMARK DOWNTOWN L.A. PROJECT COLLABORATION WITH STUDIO-MLA, OMA AND THE CITY OF LOS ANGELES

Designed to celebrate diversity and promote civic engagement, the 2-acre site will mesh art, food, and nature in the heart of the Civic Center/Grand Park area. The space will include a multi-level restaurant pavilion designed by OMA, flexible seating with canopies for shade, and a focus on native landscaping instilling awareness and sensitivity to drought and climate change. Collaborating with Studio-MLA and the City, the design team will create a signage and interpretive graphics system with a smart signage approach to enhance a connected experience to the surrounding district. Additionally, educational and interpretive signage will inform the public on noteworthy, historic or sustainable narratives, and create a world-class, integrated design that builds on the masterplan objectives.

FREE PCH TROLLEY

Doheny State Beach   The Harbor   Major Hotels
Capo Beach   Doheny Village   Lantern District

trolley.com

DANA
POINT

DANA

THE CITY OF DANA POINT
Dana Point, California

THE CITY OF DANA POINT

DANA POINT, CALIFORNIA

DANA POINT IS A COASTAL COMMUNITY WITH A POPULATION OF 30,000 THAT GROWS TO OVER 100,000 ON THE WEEKENDS

This active, picturesque playground provides residents and visitors with a myriad of recreational activities ranging from paddle boarding and kayaking to surfing and hiking. The topography of Dana Point's costal edge climbs and dips, leaving harbors and scenic plateaus along the way. With so many treasures tucked and nestled along the coastline, one would think the Pacific Coast Highway that runs through the town would provide a perfect welcome mat to tourists and visitors. However, in the past, the costal by-way has served as a pass through that left the town feeling more like a hallway than a hangout spot for visitors.

A SERIES OF COMMUNITY WORKSHOPS WITH CITY STAKEHOLDERS HELPED TO DEFINE THE CORE IMAGE OF THE CITY

Members of the city had reached out to artist Michael Schwab to create a series of banners—these pieces were used as the base of the entire project moving forward. Using the artwork as reference, it became clear how the city identified itself, and how they wanted to appear outwardly toward visitors. The team then worked to brand the city and create a series of touchpoints in the form of signage, wayfinding, collateral, a website, and a trolley. Each of these made an announcement of arrival, as well as directions to points of interest for guests.

DANA POINT

← Lantern Bay Pk
Hotel: Marriott

→ Doheny Beach

ASIDE FROM DIRECTING VISITORS, THE COMMUNITY WANTED TO MAKE ACTIVE TRANSPORTATION A PRIORITY IN THEIR WAYFINDING SYSTEM

This included conducting studies of the most walkable and bikeable paths throughout the city and then creating directionals for pedestrians alsong walkable areas. Whether it is walking from a parking space to the nearby beach, or the harbor to the downtown business district, the team worked to provide cookie crumbs of direction between different areas of the city. The town even added a public trolley system that helped to fill the longer and more challenging gaps between key destinations. The idea was to provide a complete loop that was both safe and easy to navigate with relatively little existing knowledge of the town. Creating memorable signage that serves as a road map encourages guests and residents to explore the city without the worry of getting lost or roaming too far.

OXÍGENO
Heredia, Costa Rica

OXÍGENO

HEREDIA, COSTA RICA

OXÍGENO IS MORE THAN A SPACE, A DESTINATION OR A BRAND... IT'S A LIFESTYLE

The first human playground on the planet, it is a unique and interactive space that integrates community, entertainment, sports, gastronomy, shopping, and outdoor green spaces. Aspiring to cultivate stimulating communal spaces and experiences, Oxígeno truly is a playground for the senses. Created by the people, for the people, it transcends the physical environment to become an innovative and educational tool that captures the spirit of Costa Rica as well as the community which it serves.

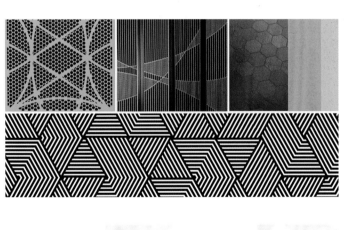

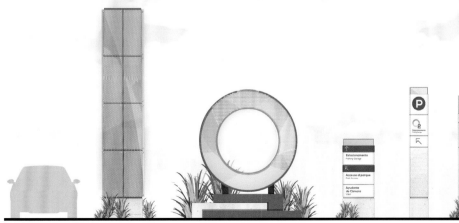

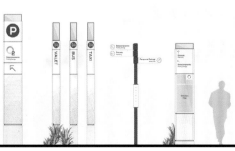

THE SHOPS AT CLEARFORK
Fort Worth, Texas

273

WAIKIKI BEACH WALK
Honolulu, Hawaii

WAIKIKI BEACH WALK

HONOLULU, HAWAII

AN NEW TRANSFORMATION OF LEWERS STREET IN DOWNTOWN WAIKIKI TO ONE OF THE LARGEST MIXED-USE DEVELOPMENTS IN THE AREA

This destination brings together international retail with the resort environment and includes five hotels, an outdoor entertainment plaza, and dozens of retailers and restaurants. The integration of lacquered hardwoods, reminiscent of historic surfboards, was incorporated to enrich the local surf history. The design included a signage program that is unique to the location by incorporating traditional Hawaiian patterns, language, song, and images throughout the project such. Iconic to the project was the inclusion of a natural stone fountain with Hawaiian lyrics, as well as educational plaques.

ʻO KA WAI LEO MŌPUA K...
E ʻALE, E KOMOHO.
...WEN?... VOICED WATER.
...ET IT RIPPLE,
LET IT RISE.
LET IT FLOW.

CODY PUEO PATA

Waikiki – The Home of Surfing

The tradition of Waikiki as a popular surfing a
unbroken since 1945. In ancient times Waikiki was a
site for Hawaiian Royalty. On certain days surfing
to members of the royal family as a privilege of their
Surfing at Waikiki experienced exponential growth
the 1940's and it is still the largest surfing ground
With Waikiki as the center, there are dozens of su
cover nearly six miles of south Oʻahu shoreline.

Waikiki is also reknown for canoe surfing.
wave forms and extreme lengths of the ride
conditions for canoe surfing.

directory**map**

hotel ↑
restaurants ↑
shops ↑
elevator →

MIAMI BAYWALK
Miami, Florida

MIAMI BAYWALK

MIAMI, FLORIDA

THE PROJECT BEGAN WITH A PRIMARY GOAL TO TRANSFORM AN UNDERUTILIZED, DISCONNECTED DESTINATION INTO ONE THAT WAS INTERNATIONALLY RECOGNIZED

In a city like Miami, the waterfront is the most valued stretch of land; it bounds neighborhoods and defines culture. The aim was to transform Miami's waterfront into a place for every person through a process that drew insights, directives, and passions directly from the public. Through a series of public outreach and design charrettes, observations were made to establish criteria for the naming, branding, and design of the overall experience.

THE DESIGN FOR MIAMI BAYWALK CONSISTS OF 16 MILES OF WALKING AND BIKING PATHS, TYING TOGETHER OVER 30 PUBLIC AND PRIVATE PROPERTIES

These paths include lighting, landscaping, hardscaping, and placemaking elements such as seating, shade, sculptures, and art which will tie together a united public space, bringing residents out to interact on their waterfront. Cultural events such as festivals, marathons, and markets are programs that the public proposed. Each component was designed for placemaking and programming, ideas that came directly from the public. Their top concerns were our immediate directives.

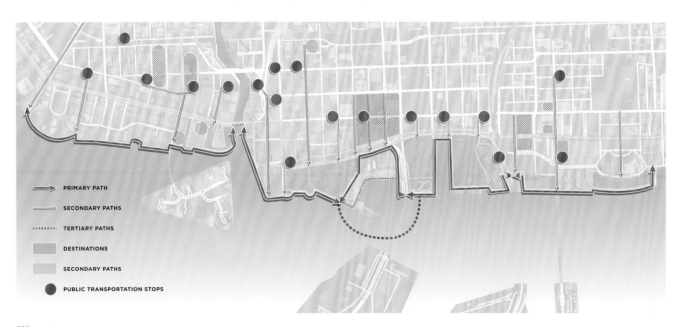

PRIMARY PATH

SECONDARY PATHS

TERTIARY PATHS

DESTINATIONS

SECONDARY PATHS

PUBLIC TRANSPORTATION STOPS

MIAMI BAYWALK WILL CREATE AN EXPERIENCE THAT WILL CELEBRATE BISCAYNE BAY AND THE RIVER'S ECOLOGY, HISTORY AND CULTURE BY CONNECTING PEOPLE TO A CONTINUOUS, VIBRANT, RESILIENT AND ICONIC WATERFRONT

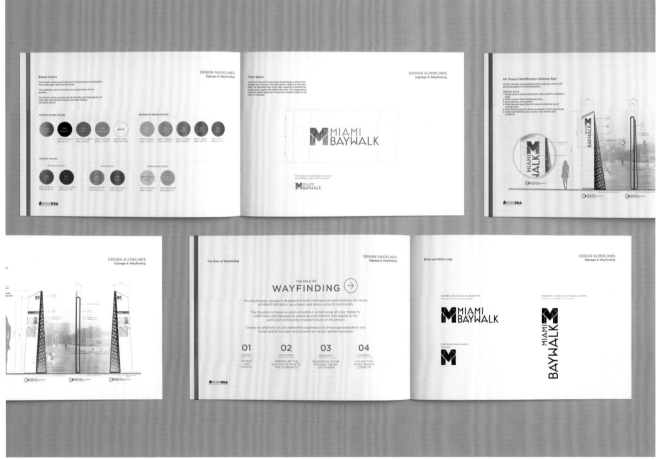

INSPIRE

CONNECTING PEOPLE TO INSPIRING PLACES WITH INTEGRITY, MEANING AND PURPOSE

Powerful design lies in creating places that inspire. These environments have an elevated sense of place that awakens us to something new and breathes life into the ordinary. There are three central ideas to bring inspiring places to life:

INTEGRITY is the idea that all the elements work together to support the big picture. Places with integrity inspire people like a well composed piece of music. Architecture, landscape design, lighting and graphics all harmonize to create a sense of place. Artful and innovative placemaking elements elevate place as a unique and memorable experience.

MEANING comes from anchoring a place to its roots. Places with meaning connect people to their heritage and culture, fosters a strong sense of identity and makes a place feel like their own. The emotional connections that come with the feeling that a place is your own is the ultimate connection to place.

PURPOSE provides a reason for a place to exist and evolve. Whether practical or infused with higher meaning, places with purpose give motivation to draw people together and engage with the environment. This sense of purpose for a place goes beyond it's typical use to elevate it's meaning within the heart of a community.

CASE STUDY

PACIFIC CITY

HUNTINGTON BEACH, CALIFORNIA

PACIFIC CITY CONNECTS PEOPLE TO PLACE AS AN INSPIRING AND ICONIC OCEANSIDE EXPERIENCE THROUGH MOMENTS OF DELIGHT AND SURPRISE

Pacific City was the original name of the early Oceanfront Village that would eventually become known as Huntington Beach. Over the span of about 7 years, the team worked with various project owners to name the project and reintroduce the historic name. The name received high praise, and the opportunity that came along with it: to take a 31-acre piece of land fronting Pacific Coast Highway, situated across from the iconic Huntington Beach Pier and Time Magazine's named "Best Beach in America", and once again bring to life a "city" with a heart and a vision for a bright future for art, leisure, creativity, community and commerce.

The project captured the heart and soul of an iconic beachfront experience by connecting the past with the present, bringing to life delightful moments that the public can engage with.

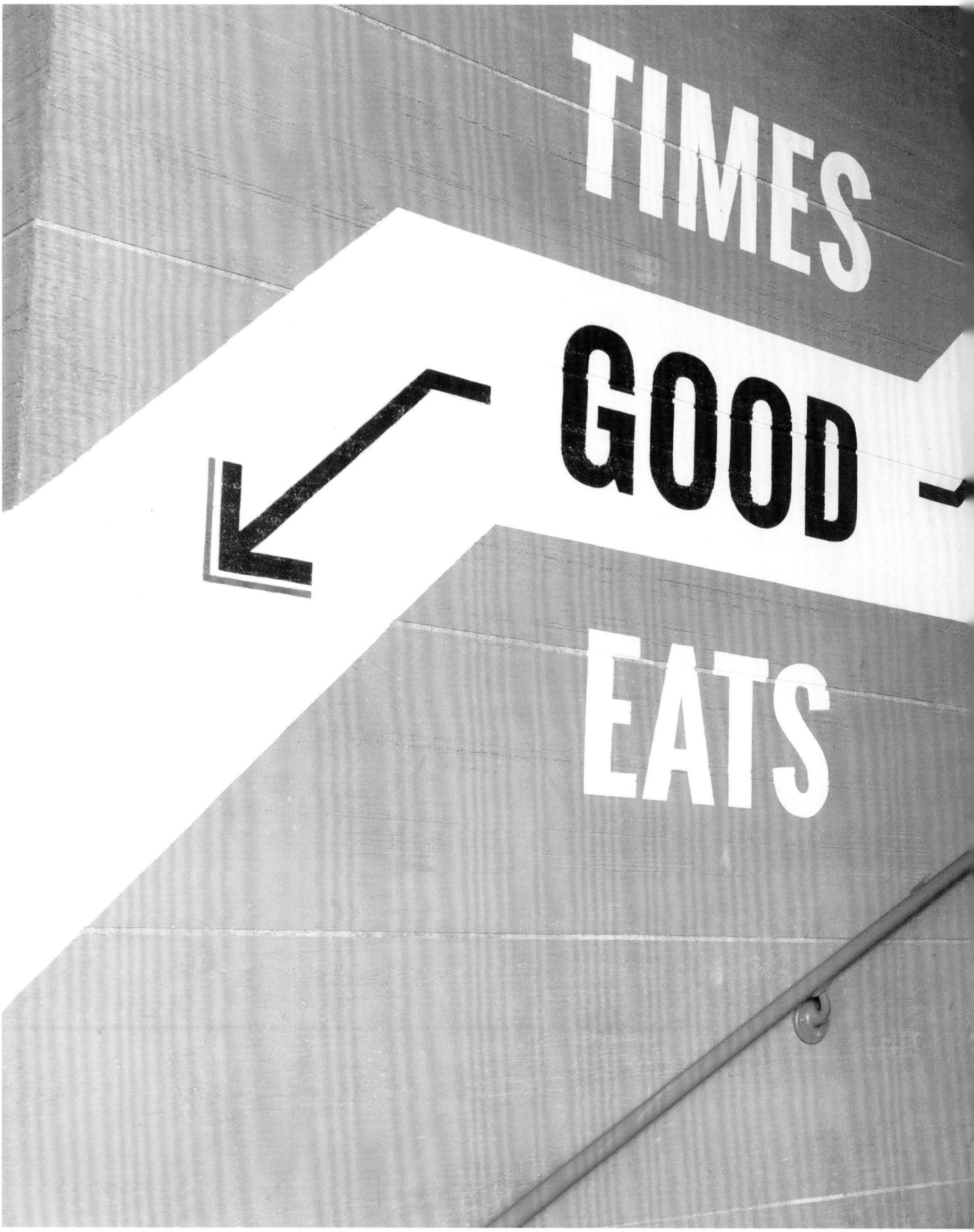
TIMES
GOOD
EATS

HISTORICAL AND CULTURAL RESEARCH HELPED TO
DISCOVER MEANINGFUL TOUCHPOINTS THAT WOULD
ENRICH THE PROJECT EXPERIENCE BY CONNECTING
PAST TO PRESENT

SURF CITY
HB MIX
COLLECTIVE
EXCHANGE
OCEAN
VILLAGE
THE BLEND
PLAZA

THE BLOCK
HB PUBLIC
COMMONS
THE UNION
BEACH CITY
SURFSIDE
**PACIFIC
CITY**

SURF NOSTALGIA
BEACH HOUSE
BLACK AND WHITE
SURF MODERN
AGAINST THE GRAIN
CANDY STRIPES
LIFE IN COLOR

DRAWING INSPIRATION FROM THE SITE AND BEACH CULTURE, A DISTINCT IDENTITY, SIGNAGE, AND WAYFINDING PROGRAM THAT CAPTURED THE UNIQUE SPIRIT OF THE PROJECT WAS CREATED

THE ARCHITECTURAL VISION WAS COMPRISED OF VILLAGE-LIKE ELEMENTS THAT COMPLEMENT THE ECLECTIC CABANA-CHIC BEACH THEME. THE TEAM WENT THE EXTRA MILE TO ENSURE BOARDS IN WOODEN WALKWAYS SQUEAK AND CREAK JUST LIKE AN AUTHENTIC PIER BOARDWALK.

Choreographing the guest experience included the process of arrival and parking, being mindful that people typically do not enjoy parking underground when going to the beach. A strategy for making the existing parking garage fun and inviting by thoughtfully studying the parking experience was put in place. The goal was to make parking less daunting, easy to navigate and in keeping with the overall experience that the larger graphics program provided.

Throughout the project—including LOT 579, an adjacent indoor food hall—designers worked to create transitional elements and temporary signage that would allow for staging and storytelling of the exciting pieces to come. The graphics that were created on barricades and temporary signage became such a beloved part of the experience that the public demanded them back, wondering where they had gone after the space had been further developed.

The temporary graphics returned as permanent graphics. Visitors still flock to these graphic elements as places where classic Instagram moments come to life.

TEMPORARY GRAPHICS BECAME PERMANENT PLACEMAKING ELEMENTS THAT HAVE BECOME INTEGRAL TO THE PACIFIC CITY EXPERIENCE

THE RESIDENCES AT PACIFIC CITY

Huntington Beach, California

THE RESIDENCES AT PACIFIC CITY

HUNTINGTON BEACH, CALIFORNIA

THE RESIDENCES AT PACIFIC CITY ARE CLASSICALLY DESIGNED, HIGH-QUALITY HOMES, NESTLED WITHIN A THRIVING NEW RESTAURANT AND BOUTIQUE SHOPPING SCENE

RSM Design created a brand identity, designed an interior and exterior signage vocabulary, developed a public art program, and conducted a study of the wayfinding and sign placement program throughout the site. The design inspiration for the project was a sophisticated, simplified, beach-town feeling capturing the beauty of the natural landscape. The signage system marries the simple logomark with warm, natural materials and creates a restrained echo of the surroundings.

FOUR

LEVEL 1
4103–4108

LEVEL 2
4201–4208

LEVEL 3
4301–4308

LEVEL 4
4401–4411

LIBERTY STATION
San Diego, California

LIBERTY STATION

SAN DIEGO, CALIFORNIA

LIBERTY STATION IS ABOUT INSPIRED MOMENTS... THE SPONTANEOUS AND VIBRANT EXPERIENCES THAT LEAVE LASTING IMPRESSIONS WHERE DISCOVERY IS ORGANIC AND AUTHENTICITY IS LIVED NOT INVENTED

The mission of every project is to curate unique opportunities for fellowship, connection and community to flourish. A unique space that juxtaposes the essence of the projects historical influence with the innate authenticity of the various districts to create a holistic experience. A place where people come time and again to be connected, engaged and will call their own.

LIBERTY STATION

SAN DIEGO, CALIFORNIA

HISTORY

While many associate the anchor with the
navy, we see it as a source of strength.
Like an anchor our historic roots have laid
a firm foundation upon which we look to build
the future. It provides stability, a steady hold
and hope as we set out on new adventures.

FUTURE

Innovation is our guiding light and north star.
While we are rooted in the past our vision
is set on the future. Just as man has admired
the night sky and aspired to reach the stars,
we strive to make the impossible possible.

COMMUNITY

The circle represents connection.
An endless ring that conjures the love
of place, community, and commitment.
It's where memories are made, and friendships
are formed. An inclusive destination where
everyone feels welcome, safe and united.

LIBERTY STATION

SAN DIEGO, CALIFORNIA

VICTORIA GARDENS MONET AVENUE
Rancho Cucamonga, California

VICTORIA GARDENS MONET AVENUE

RANCHO CUCAMONGA, CALIFORNIA

MONET AVENUE IS A TWO BLOCK STREET LOCATED WITHIN THE LARGER VICTORIA GARDENS SHOPPING DISTRICT

In an effort to revitalize the area to match the vibrancy of the rest of the neighborhood, Forest City set off on a repositioning effort to improve circulation and fill unrenewed leases. The design team was asked to create a system of creative placemaking signage and wayfinding for the two block street that would complement the existing signage. The family of signs included new interpretive signage and directories, as well as various wall-mounted directionals. A collection of environmental graphics was also created, and included colorful crosswalks and paving details.

336

HOFGARTEN
SOLINGEN

HOFGARTEN
Solingen, Germany

HOFGARTEN

SOLINGEN, GERMANY

AT HOFGARTEN IN SOLINGEN, GERMANY YOU CAN SHOP ACCORDING TO YOUR MOOD AND PERSONAL STYLE

You will find everything that makes up the complete shopping experience. Hofgarten plays with modern architecture, designing with the themes of "nature, industry and fashion" in mind. Inspired by the "City of Knives," The team developed a truly cutting edge sign package perfect for the center. Clean, innovative, playful, futuristic, and electric, taking environmental graphics to another level and creating a unique lifestyle experience for those who visit.

AN EMPHASIS WAS PLACED ON LAYERED TEXTURES AND PATTERNS

THE MARTIN
San Francisco, California

THE MARTIN

SAN FRANCISCO, CALIFORNIA

THE MARTIN IS A STYLISH AND ACTIVE NON-CONFORMIST WHO REVELS IN THE ART OF ENJOYING THE GOOD THINGS IN LIFE

Career-minded and life-loving, The Martin is built around the history and culture of the Dogpatch, "a small town in a big city." The Martin is a 92-apartment luxury residential building. It is designed with the entrepreneur, artist, and creative in mind. With eclectic touches and state of the art features, The Martin is named after the Martin Brothers Shipping Company which formerly occupied the project site. The Martin, offers unobstructed bay views, waterfront access, and close proximity to one of the nations strongest job markets, downtown San Francisco.

NEWPORT BEACH, CA | EST. 1971

LIDO MARINA

VILLAGE

LIDO MARINA VILLAGE
Newport Beach, California

LIDO MARINA VILLAGE

NEWPORT BEACH, CALIFORNIA

LIDO MARINA VILLAGE, LOCATED ON BALBOA PENINSULA IN NEWPORT BEACH, IS A CASUAL WATERSIDE RETAIL AND DINING DESTINATION HAVING RECENTLY UNDERGONE A COMPLETE REVITALIZATION

The design team worked with DJM Capital Partners to reimagine the property as a high-end shopping and gathering destination for Orange County. The simple and casual branded environment contributed to a fresh aesthetic that guides visitors through the project. Utlizing a nautical palette of high gloss teak wood with accents of polished brass to visually connect to the adjacent docks, boats, and harbor. A simple palette of black, white, and dark grey painted throughout the project creates a timeless seaside feel that compliments the architectural style.

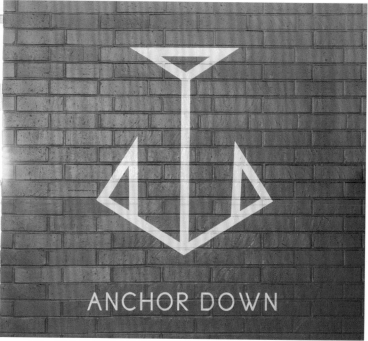

LONG BEACH EXCHANGE
Long Beach, California

LONG BEACH EXCHANGE

LONG BEACH, CALIFORNIA

LBX IS AN EXPERIENTIAL RETAIL AND DINING DESTINATION NEIGHBORING THE LONG BEACH INTERNATIONAL AIRPORT IN SOUTHERN CALIFORNIA

LBX encompasses approximately 266,000 square feet of restaurant and retail space. The project scope included the overall project signage, wayfinding and specialty graphics, as well as tenant signage and graphics for the artisan food hall, The Hangar. The goals of these elements were to enhance visibility, express brand identity, and provide unique "Instagram Moments" through placemaking and graphic interventions. The project's proximity to the airport inspired the fun and colorful air travel-inspired designs.

rsmdesign

RSM DESIGN TEAM

It is only through the creative and inspired efforts of individuals, teams and collaborators working together that make innovative design and engaging projects possible. RSM Design would like to thank all the collaborators that have helped make the work presented in this book a reality.

Alexandra Abramson	Jaime Gonzalez	Sydney Patterson
Leslie Alleshouse	Laura Goodrow	Nicole Perez
Stefanie Ashton	Claire Grifffin	Sage Peterson
Elva Avila	Alicia Hanson	Vince Peterson
Ashley Ayres	Michael Hanson	Josh Petty
Wendy Belt	Gregory Hastings	Lorraine Ramero
Brieann Berg	Erin Hatfield	Julia Rapport
Tyler Bickel	Adam Hayes	Georgia Redmond
Elizabeth Bodzy	Rhonda Headley	Steve Reinisch
Emily Boelsems	Will Heinze	Holly Richardson
Christine Brady	Maxwell Helm	Kyle Richter
Anna Brink	Jeffrey Hertzler	Tatiana Rodriguez
Eric Bro	Anthony Hilger	Santiogo Sada de la Paz
Susan Burckle	Tory Hoffman	Janie Savadra
Ross Burdekin	Katie Hollman	Eddie Sayers
Zack Burson	Steve Hopper	Elliott Schwartz
Nathanie Cabrera	Alyx House	Katharine Schwartz
MacKenna Carney	Chao Chi Huang	Martin Schwartz
Jason Carulli	Deborah Hughes	Suzanne R. Schwartz
Darlene Casco	Ali Mohammed Imarni	William Schwartz
Marianne Caupers	Michael Johansen	Yolanda Sepulveda
Cathleen Chamness	Nikki Johnson	Alyssa Shapkoff
Laura Chevalier	Hanna Kahn	Josephine Shaw
Samantha Choo	Michael Kaiser	Sophie Shaw
Cody Clark	Dyna Kau	Juan Sierra
Susan Clark	Steven Kelly	Taylor Silver
Cory Clinton	Katherine Labadie	Jerome Solano
KK Closuit	Jeff Lancaster	David Stein
Jill Cole	David Lee	Kelly Stewart
Alex Cooper	Ron Leland	Lisa Surman
Lisa Cronin	Daniel Lopes	Thom Surman
Laura Cunningham	Kathleen Malouf	Jason Sweers
Simone Drucker	Harry Mark	DJ Thomas
Kelly Ehrheart	Alexandra Martin	Sue Tunstall
Scott Eichler	Steve Martin	Jake Warner
Kelley Eldridge	Bradley Mathais	Alec White
Erin Ellison	Marcia Maynes	Carolyn Wilder
Laura Escarcega	Keaton McCalla	Matt Williams
Aaron Ferber	Mary McGraw	Leah Willis
Landon Fisher	Max McIlwee	Stephanie Wills
Derek Friday	Cody Meeks	Xian Wong
Catherine Gardener	Erica Mendel	Leon Wood
Michelle Garrido	Valerie Mendivil	Carly Zembrodt
Graham Gaylor	Christy Montgomery	Zuzanna Zohar
Kate Gilman	Izzy Oedekerk	Ashley Zwar
Scott Gleason	Eloisa Ortiz	

IMAGE CREDITS

For a complete list of credits, please visit our website at rsmdesign.com.

AJ Alao on Unsplash
Allison Richter Photography
Andrew Buchanan on Unsplash
Andrew Ridley on Unsplash
Arlen Kennedy
Aziz J.Hayat on Unsplash
Benoy
Boy Scouts of America Flickr
Callison/Chris Eden
Carlos Lindler on Unsplash
Civic Arts
Cody McLain on Unsplash
Dallas News
Daniel Hansen on Unsplash
David Lauer Photography
Dmitri Popov on Unsplash
Donald Satterlee
Emaar Properties
Etty Fidele on Unsplash
From MVE
Furuta Family Archives
Gabriel Santiago on Unsplash
Gary Hartley
Gensler
Google Maps
Graphic Burger
HPP Architekten GmbH
Instagram Contributors
Ivanhoe Cambridge
Jack Tindall on Unsplash
Jakob Owens on Unsplash
James Baldwin on Unsplash
Jerde
John Draper
Jonnu Singleton
Karen Lau on Unsplash
Kristin Wilson

Lara Swimmer
LEPAA
Lynn Donovan
MacKenzi Martin on Unsplash
Mat Reding on Unsplash
Miami Design District Website
Michael Cagle, LLC
Michael Silkesjoo on Unsplash
Monica Ramos Style Blogger
Muzammil Soorma on Unsplash
Nikolay Tarashchenko on Unsplash
Nova Partners
Omniplan
Peter Calvin
Phillip Pessar
Robert Metz on Unsplash
Robert Zunikoff on Unsplash
Samuel Zeller on Unsplash
Savino Miller Design
SB Architects
Scott Lewis
Sergey Koznov on Unsplash
Shutterstock
Smith Group
Stir Architecture
Studio Match
Studio MLA
Sven Read on Unsplash
The Beck Group
The Martin Website
Tichnor Brothers Postcard Collection
Trent Haaland on Unsplash
Tsutsumida Pictures
UC Riverside Today
UOP, Arthur A. Dugoni School of Dentistry
ZSun Fu on Unsplash
贝莉儿 NG on Unsplash